Our Mother's TABLE

THE *Culinary* JOURNEY *of* BENEVA MAYWEATHER

How do we say goodbye? Do we really have to?

Let our memories keep the spirit of our loved ones alive in our hearts.

This book is dedicated to our mother, Beneva Bone Mayweather, and to all mothers who love their children unconditionally and who never tire of nourishing their bodies as well as their hearts.

Emma, Patricia, Eva and Cynthia

Our
Mother's
TABLE

THE *Culinary* JOURNEY
of BENEVA MAYWEATHER

Written by:
Emma Mayweather Lincoln
Denise Sims

Photographs by:
Ann Bullard
Mary Ehrhart
Ben Fink
Dottie Sanders

Graphic Design:
Patterson Graham

Illustration / Art Direction:
Jean Holmgren

Foreward

*From the fields of Arkansas, to life in Detroit and then Memphis, the journey
that Beneva Bone Mayweather took to become one of the most celebrated caterers in the
Mid-South is a story in itself. From the simplest dish to the most extravagant spread,
the methods and preparation changed,
but the honesty and love of cooking remained the same.*

Her entry into the world of catering began when she was a very young woman
working as a cook at the Memphis (Tennessee) Hunt and Polo Club. Initially, her responsibilities
were limited to light assignments, but after watching those around her and studying all that she
could, she mastered the necessary techniques to earn a spot as a chef.

Her legendary abilities did not go unnoticed, and demands for her culinary talents
increased. From those humble beginnings, a business was born. Her company, Beneva
Mayweather Catering, Inc., not only lifted the name of this remarkable woman to great
heights, but it set a new benchmark for catering service in Memphis society that
remains the standard of excellence to this very day.

Our Mother's Table is a tribute to our mother, Beneva Mayweather, and to her
memory we dedicate this book. There is no way that we can list each individual
who contributed in some way, but we can say a collective "thank you" to all who had a part
in the project and gave their support.

It was an experience we will never forget. We talked with family members, friends,
co-workers and club members. We visited the Arkansas home site and pored through
old pictures and family mementos. We sat with our father and pulled from our own
wonderful memories the warmth, caring and honesty that was our mother.

We laughed, we cried and we celebrated a life so well lived.
It was as if we were once again…at our Mother's table.

Table of Contents

5

Introduction

The eastern part of Arkansas was given the gift of Delta culture and graciousness by the Mississippi River. The water's winding, flowing pattern etched natural boundaries which separated states and cities, but its unbelievable history created a region - a region which gave birth to Southern traditions, Southern roots.

Across the portion of the river running along southwest Tennessee and northern Mississippi was a fertile part of Arkansas where families worked the land, raised crops, kept livestock and lived a rural life. The area was beautiful, with wild flowers and grassy fields, and although it offered a natural, wholesome environment, it also brought to light the reality of farm life with its constant care of the land and its inevitable hard work.

Within this environment, our mother was born. The seventh of nine children, Beneva Patricia Bone learned early the importance of love and family. The Bones of Lexa, Arkansas were a close-knit family, admired and respected throughout the community. They lived on and owned 75 acres in Lexa, a little community just outside of West Helena. Like the Bones, most of the people in that area were African-American farmers whose lives and livelihoods alike were inextricably tied to the land. And although they depended on the land, they were a strong, determined people who believed that they and their children were an integral part of a much bigger world, and that their contributions to that world would touch many.

They believed in education. In rural Arkansas, like in so many small areas throughout the South during that time, the school year revolved around the needs of the land. Young people were expected to help with planting, tilling the soil, and later, gathering the crops. Often, students - particularly young African-American students - were unable to attend classes during certain parts of the year. Many did not go past grammar school; others went only a few years into the higher grades. The Bones, like others in that small community, were proud people who believed in education. Their children attended Rosenwald Grade School (one of the Rosenwald schools built for African-American children in the early part of the century) and Southland College (later called Walter Southland), a Quaker school for which their father, Albert Bone, paid up to twenty dollars each month for each child's tuition.

At Rosenwald, and at Walter Southland, young Beneva was known as a good student who excelled in all her subjects. It was at Walter Southland that she won several competitions in oratory and speech, earning a trip to Washington, D.C. with her instructors to compete with students from all across the country. It was this exposure, along with her self-determination, that helped to define her character. And, despite the limitations of segregation and denial facing her at the time, she maintained a sense of high standards and a can-do attitude that she carried with her for the rest of her life. This love of learning would be instilled later in her four daughters, who understood their mother's passion and who attained high academic achievements.

As she grew, she also discovered that education was just one of the things that she dearly loved. Beneva loved to watch as her mother cared for her family, paying careful attention to how she prepared the three meals they enjoyed each day. Indeed, it was from her mother, Essie, that she learned to cook, and the recipes that she would rely upon for decades were variations of her mother's culinary skills.

Interestingly enough, an early incident in her childhood home laid the groundwork for young Beneva's future calling. One day, when her mother and grandmother were away, she began preparing the meals for that day. Happy to take her mother's place in the kitchen, her eagerness soon took a different direction, and she realized she was not as prepared as she thought. Having cooked the food too early in the day, Beneva attempted to keep it warm. Warming for such a long period of time however caused the meal to burn and she became despondent. So, how wonderful it was that a loving family could understand the meal before them and yet smile while wondering what the food was and what it had been! And, how fortunate it was that she learned from that mistake, and that she went on to become one of the most beloved chefs and caterers in the Memphis area!

In her honor, this collection of Beneva's favorite recipes, as well as recipes shared by family and friends, is presented within the chapters of her life. Food and the events of living combine to make a natural association. Remember birthdays? Surprise parties? The holidays? Remember the fun, the friendship - the food? The times of our lives are carefully locked in our memories, and in our memories are the wonders of breaking bread together. Our mother understood this, and each meal, party and event that she catered carried with it a special touch that only she could deliver.

This is the story of Beneva Bone Mayweather's culinary journey, from the cotton fields of Lexa, Arkansas to the board rooms of Memphis, Tennessee. This is her story - through food, through family and through love.

Down HOME

In the 1930s and 40s in rural eastern Arkansas, life was simple - a reflection of the times. Winter meant cold, rainy weather, but it also meant long nights with family, short days in school and thoughts of planting to come.

Spring was the emergence of seed, the beauty of wildflowers and the warmth of the gentle sun. Summer meant splashes in the nearby pond, long sunny days and freedom from schoolwork. Autumn rounded out the cycle with pumpkin and cranberry sunsets, cool evenings and hints of frost.

For a young Beneva Bone, those were the kind and gentle days of youth. Those days soon evolved into days of adolescence, where fun became work and where the joy of youth became the reality of adult responsibility. The seasons, with all their glory, now meant preparing the livestock for winter slaughter, tilling the damp fields for new gardens, bringing in the crops from the heat of the sun and canning the bounty of the family's labor.

These are the ingredients of what Southerners call "DOWN HOME" a reference that is made with respect and love.

Beneva rose early, milking cows, tending to the garden, and joining her parents, sisters and brothers in the fields, picking and chopping endless crops of cotton for market.

But despite the times, the needs and the realities of life in Arkansas during the 1930s and '40s, young Beneva emerged as sturdy and beautiful as the wildflowers she so dearly loved. She relished the Sunday dinners with the members of the Bone family. She waited each summer for the church picnics that brought promise of fun and good food. She loved the sounds and the smells of the country holidays that never failed to warm the spirit and bring people together. These are the ingredients of what Southeners call "Down Home" a reference that is made with respect and love.

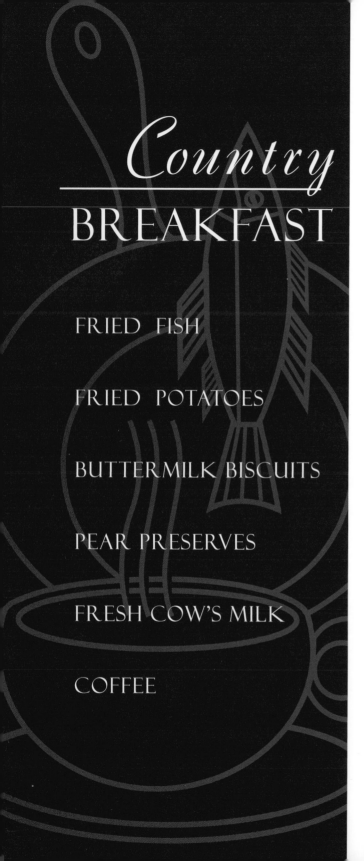

Country
BREAKFAST

FRIED FISH

FRIED POTATOES

BUTTERMILK BISCUITS

PEAR PRESERVES

FRESH COW'S MILK

COFFEE

In years past, the breakfast meal was a hardy, satisfying meal. It served a dual purpose - one, it followed a long night of sleeping since bedtime was much earlier, and two, it prepared the family for the heavy morning work to come.

The cured meats of winter meant tasty ham and bacon. The canned fruits of summer meant preserves, jams and jellies. In the South, these were the makings of breakfast, and they joined grits, eggs, potatoes and biscuits as the ingredients for a morning meal.

And let's not forget Arkansas' favorite - rice! The low, wetlands throughout the state were perfect for growing this most popular staple of the South. Whether covered with gravy, smothered with butter or served alone, it was often part of a morning meal that sent everybody on their way.

That is what made this Southern meal so unique - foods that many considered to be suitable for a dinner menu were served at breakfast! Luckily it wasn't so strange for our mother's family. In fact, it was down right good!

Fried
FISH

Ingredients:
4-6 Pieces Catfish or Buffalo
Salt
Black Pepper
Red Pepper
Yellow Corn Meal
Peanut Oil
*Hint: For children and some adults, boneless catfish is better,
although all fish should be checked for small bones.*

Directions:
Lightly sprinkle each side of the fish with salt, black pepper and red
pepper. Roll both sides of fish in yellow corn meal.

Fill a third of the skillet with peanut oil, and heat over medium heat.
(To test heat, drop a pinch of meal into oil.
If the meal sizzles, the oil is hot enough to fry.)

Fry fish a few minutes on each side until golden brown.
Drain on paper towels. Serve hot.
Makes 4 to 6 servings.

Buttermilk
BISCUITS

Ingredients:
2 Cups Sifted All-Purpose Flour
3 Teaspoons Baking Powder
1/2 Teaspoon Salt
1 Pinch Baking Soda
1/2 Cup Vegetable Shortening
1 Cup Buttermilk

Directions:
Preheat oven to 350 degrees. Stir dry ingredients into a large bowl. Cut in shortening with a fork. Blend in the buttermilk quickly until dry ingredients are moistened.

Turn onto lightly floured surface (dough should be soft), and knead gently with about 10 strokes. (Do not work the dough any more - biscuits will be tough.) Lightly dust a rolling pin with flour and roll dough 1/2 inch thick. Dip biscuit cutter in flour; push cutter straight down into dough. (Use a 2 1/2" or 3" biscuit cutter.)

Bake on lightly greased baking sheet at 350 degrees about 12 minutes. Yields approximately 12 biscuits.

Fried POTATOES

Ingredients:
4 Medium or 3 Large Red Potatoes
1 Large Onion, Chopped
1/4 Cup Cooking Oil
Salt
Pepper

Directions:
Peel potatoes and cut into cubes (you may shred potatoes if you like a crunchier dish). Rinse and drain potatoes.

Heat the oil, add the onions, and cook until soft but not browned. Over medium high heat, add the potatoes, stirring occasionally to keep them from sticking. (You may add a tablespoon of water to steam the potatoes a bit, but they will not be as crunchy.)

Cover and cook over low heat until done.
Salt and pepper to taste.
Makes 4 to 6 servings.

Pear
PRESERVES

Ingredients:

4 to 5 Very Firm Pears (when sliced, enough to fill a quart jar)
2 Tablespoons Lemon Juice
1 1/2 Cups Sugar
Jar with a Seal (for Canning)

Directions:

Wash the pears; drain thoroughly. Core, peel, and slice into thick sections.
Put in a large bowl, sprinkle with the lemon juice, and toss gently.
Totally cover the fruit with sugar, refrigerate, and let stand overnight.
The mixture will make its own juice.

In a large saucepan, bring the sugar and pear mixture to a boil, carefully stirring every few minutes. Lower the heat and simmer until the fruit is tender and the juice is thick. Carefully pour into a hot sterilized jar. Wipe the edges of the jar with a paper towel or a clean cloth and seal.

Hint: You may use hard, "country pears" often found at open–air or farmers' markets, or through mail-order services.

Fresh COW'S MILK

Ingredients:

If early morning milking is not your cup of tea, pick up one carton of your favorite brand - fresh from the store!

As we hurry home from our places of work, or as we plan our activities for the end of the day, we consider "dinner" as a meal eaten around six or seven in the evening. As Beneva came of age in rural Arkansas, "dinner" was the midday meal at which families ate what we now consider "the meat and threes." Home grown vegetables, roasted meats, desserts, buttered rolls and breads all graced tables in the early afternoon sun, a welcome and wonderful break from hours of work.

An added treat came when Papa Albert came home from hunting. Beneva and her brothers and sisters knew that dinner would soon mean a dish of squirrel, rabbit or other game readily found around the area. In today's times, the selection seems less than palatable, but for many families, a platter of game was considered special. Properly prepared, it was looked upon as a delicacy and was especially popular at family gatherings and social events. It represented the unique ability of people of that time to live from the land, simply yet creatively.

❖

Middle
OF THE DAY
DINNER

SMOTHERED RABBIT

MIXED TURNIP AND MUSTARD GREENS

FRIED GREEN TOMATOES

CANDIED SWEET POTATOES

BEETS AND ONIONS

CRACKLING BREAD

BREAD PUDDING WITH BOURBON SAUCE

Smothered
RABBIT

Ingredients:
1 Rabbit (available in some grocery stores and meat markets)
Salt
Pepper
Flour
Cooking Oil
Water

Directions:
Have the rabbit cleaned and cut into serving pieces (if not purchased this way). Soak meat in salted water overnight. Drain meat and blot dry. Lightly salt and pepper both sides of meat, then flour both sides. Coat the bottom of a frying pan with oil; raise to medium heat. Carefully place rabbit pieces in the frying pan and cook until browned on both sides. Remove to a roasting pan.

Without turning off the frying pan, add two heaping tablespoons of flour, stirring constantly so that the flour browns in the pan drippings. Once it begins to brown, slowly add one cup of water stirring constantly. When the liquid thickens, lower heat and continue to cook until it has gravy consistency. Season to taste. Turn off heat.

Preheat oven to 350 degrees. Pour gravy over the rabbit pieces, cover tightly with a lid or with foil and cook for one hour or until tender. Spoon gravy over the smothered rabbit when serving. Makes 2 to 4 servings.

Mixed Turnip &
MUSTARD GREENS

Ingredients:
2 Large Bunches Mustard Greens (or 1 pound)
2 Large Bunches Turnip Greens
1 Piece Salt Pork (about 4 ounces)*
2 Teaspoon Crushed Red Pepper
1 Teaspoon Sugar
Salt to Taste

*Can substitute salt pork with smoked turkey wings

Directions:
Pick and remove stems from greens. In a sink, wash greens 2-3 times
in cold water. Boil salt pork in 6 to 8 cups of water for approximately
30 minutes. Add greens and the red pepper to the pot and boil
approximately 30 minutes to an hour until tender. (Less tender
greens may take longer.) Add 1 teaspoon of sugar. (If a fresh red
pepper pod is used, remember to remove before serving.)
Makes 4 to 6 servings.

Note: In many parts of the south, greens are sold by the bunch. In some areas,
they are sold by the pound. A good rule of thumb to remember is that greens
"cook down" and one bunch or pound makes plentiful servings for two people.

Fried
GREEN
TOMATOES

Ingredients:
3 Green Tomatoes, Unpeeled
Salt and Pepper
1/2 Cup Flour
1 Cup Plain Corn Meal
2 Eggs
1/2 Cup Milk
1/2 Cup Oil
1/2 Cup Butter
Additional Salt and Pepper to taste

Directions:
Wash and slice tomatoes. Salt and pepper the tomato slices. In a separate pan or bowl, mix together flour and corn meal and set aside. Beat eggs and milk together. Dip tomato slices into egg and milk, then into flour and meal mixture. Heat oil and butter in a large skillet and brown the tomato slices on both sides, turning with a spatula only once to prevent breaking. Remove and drain on paper towels. Makes about 10 to 12 slices.

Candied
SWEET
POTATOES

Ingredients:

4 Medium Sweet Potatoes
1 Cup Sugar
1 Cup Water
1 Stick Butter (1/4 pound)
2 Oranges, Sliced Thin
Juice of 1 lemon

Directions:

Preheat oven to 350 degrees. Peel potatoes and slice (about 3/4 to an inch thick). Wash in a bowl of water and lemon juice (to prevent darkening). Pour off water. Make a simple syrup by combining the water and sugar. Boil until the sugar dissolves, add the butter. Arrange the potatoes in a baking dish. Place an orange slice over each potato slice. Pour the syrup over the potatoes, cover and let bake for an hour or until tender.
Makes about 4 to 6 servings.

Beets &
ONIONS

Ingredients:
6 to 8 Fresh Beets
1 Large White or Yellow Onion, Sliced
1/2 Cup White Vinegar
1/4 Cup Sugar
3/4 Cup Water

Directions:
Wash and trim beets, cover with water and boil until tender. Remove from water and let cool. Slip off skin and cut into medium sized slices. In a serving bowl, layer the beets and the onions. In a saucepan heat the vinegar, sugar and water until the sugar is dissolved. Pour over the vegetables. Place the bowl in the refrigerator and let set for several hours or overnight. Serve chilled.
Makes 6 generous servings.

Crackling BREAD
(Cornbread)

Ingredients:
2 Cups Plain Corn Meal
1/2 Cup Flour
1/2 Teaspoon Baking Powder
1/2 Teaspoon Salt
2 Tablespoons Sugar
Pinch of Baking Soda
1 Cup Buttermilk
2 Tablespoons Oil

Directions:
Preheat oven to 375 degrees.

Mix dry ingresdients together; add milk and oil.
Stir in crackling. Pour batter into greased skillet.
Bake in hot oven until browned (About 25 minutes)

Let cool five minutes before serving.
Serves 6 to 8.

Bread
PUDDING *with Bourbon Sauce*

Ingredients:

1 Cup Raisins	3 Cups Milk
Boiling Water	1 Cup Light Cream
10-12 Slices of Bread, Buttered	1 Long Curl of Lemon Peel
1 1/2 Cups Sugar	4 Eggs, Lightly Beaten
Ground Cinnamon	

Directions:

Preheat oven to 325 degrees. Place raisins in a bowl and plump by covering with boiling water for 2-3 minutes; drain the raisins. Remove the crusts from the bread slices, and cut each slice lengthwise into three pieces. Place a layer of bread strips, buttered side up, in the bottom of a greased shallow baking dish (1 1/2 quarts). Lightly sprinkle with cinnamon, then sprinkle with 1/3 of the raisins and one tablespoon of sugar. Repeat with another layer of bread, cinnamon, raisins, and sugar until the dish is half full and there are three complete layers.

Heat the milk, cream, lemon peel, and the remaining sugar until boiling. Slowly add the boiling mixture to the eggs while stirring constantly to prevent the eggs from cooking. Slowly pour the egg mixture over the bread. Allow to stand 30 minutes before baking.

Set the baking dish in a deep pan, and pour simmering water around the dish. Bake for an hour or until the custard is set and the top becomes browned and crusty. Remove the pudding from the water bath. Serve warm or cold.

Makes 4 to 6 dessert servings.

"See Next Page" FOR THE SAUCE.

Bourbon Sauce

Ingredients:
1 Cup Milk
1/2 Cup Half & Half
1/2 Cup Butter
1 Cup Sugar
3 Tablespoons Cornstarch
1/4 Cup Water
1/2 Cup Bourbon

Directions:
Cook milk, half & half, butter, and sugar in
a heavy saucepan over low heat,
stirring constantly until butter
melts and sugar dissolves.

Combine cornstarch and water, stirring until
smooth. Add to butter mixture, stir in bourbon. Bring mixture to a boil over medium
heat, stirring constantly about 1 minute. Pour
over pudding before serving. May be served
warm or cold.

Light SUPPER

HOE CAKE

SALT PORK (STREAK O'LEAN)

Listening to the radio...sitting quietly on the side porch... going over late evening homework to get ready for school . . . .

These were the makings of evenings for young Beneva. A quiet time, a reflective time, it was a time for the calm of twilight and the expectation of tomorrow. The heavier meals of the day gave way to lighter fare - to a "hoecake" and sorghum, or to a small portion of leftovers from dinner.

A quiet time, a reflective time, it was a time for the calm of twilight and the expectation of tomorrow.

Hoe CAKE

Ingredients:
Leftover Biscuit Dough from Breakfast
(see page 14 or page 147)
Or Leftover Dough from Rolls
(see page 186)
Oil

Directions:
Take the leftover biscuit dough (or leftover dough from rolls)
and form small patties 3 to 4 inches in diameter.
Over medium high heat, brown the "cakes" on both sides in a lightly
greased skillet. Can be eaten with molasses, preserves, or jellies.

Salted Pork (STREAK O'LEAN)

Ingredients:
1 Pound of Salt Pork (sliced medium)
Water
Oil

Directions:
Cover sliced pork with water and boil 5 to 10 minutes. Remove
and place on paper towels to drain. Fry in vegetable oil (enough
to coat skillet). Drain and serve.

Sunday DINNER

BAKED CHICKEN

FAMILY BEEF ROAST

MASHED POTATOES

SMOTHERED CABBAGE

FRIED CORN

SPOON BREAD

HOMEMADE VANILLA
ICE CREAM

POUND CAKE

Solid as the monument it is, the family Sunday dinner remains a shrine to women and men everywhere who relish making a meal that everyone appreciates. Combine food, family and friends, and you have an enviable afternoon of love, warmth and joy.

Baked
CHICKEN

Ingredients:
1 Whole Chicken Cut into Quarters
Vegetable Oil
Salt
Pepper
Paprika
1 Stick (a quater pound) Butter, Melted
1 Cup Water

Directions:
Rub chicken with oil and place in a baking pan or dish. Sprinkle chicken with salt, pepper and paprika. Pour melted butter over chicken. Pour 1 cup of water in pan.

Cook at 350 degrees for 25 to 30 minutes until brown and tender. Makes 4 servings.

Family
ROAST BEEF

Ingredients:

2-3 Pound Beef Chuck Roast
Salt
Pepper
1/4 Cup Oil

1 Yellow Onion, Sliced
1/2 Cup Water
2 White Potatoes
2 Large Carrots

Directions:

Rinse beef, season with salt and pepper on both sides. Heat oil in skillet; brown the roast quickly on both sides. Reserve drippings.

Place roast, along with the drippings, in a roasting pan. Place sliced onions on top of the meat. Add water, cover and bake at 350 degrees for 1 1/2 hours.

Peel, wash, and slice potatoes and carrots. Place carrots and potatoes around roast, cover, and return to the oven for another hour or until done.

Serves 4 to 6.

Mashed
POTATOES

Ingredients:
6 Large Red Potatoes
1 Stick of Butter
Salt
White Pepper
Half & Half

Directions:
Peel the 6 red potatoes. Cut the potatoes into cube shapes, and then rinse and drain. In a saucepan, cover the potatoes with cold water, bring to a boil, and cook the potatoes until they are well done. Drain the potatoes.

Put the potatoes into a mixing bowl. Add 1 stick of butter. Add salt and pepper to taste. Add half and half to the mixing bowl while mashing the potatoes until the desired consistency is obtained. Makes 4 to 6 servings.

Smothered CABBAGE

Ingredients:
1 Head of Cabbage
3 to 4 Slices Bacon
1/2 Cup of Water
1/2 Cup Chopped Onions
Salt
Pepper
1 Tablespoon Cracked Red Pepper

Directions:
Rinse and shred cabbage. Heat a skillet and fry 3 to 4 pieces of bacon. Remove bacon, leaving the drippings.
To the skillet add the shredded cabbage and 1/2 cup of water. Sprinkle onions into cabbage. Cook on high heat, stirring frequently. Add cracked red pepper and seasonings to taste. Serves 4 to 6.

Note: Remove from heat before leaves wilt!

Fried

CORN

Ingredients:
8 Ears of Corn
1 Stick of Butter
1 Tablespoon Sugar
1 Teaspoon Salt
1 Tablespoon Flour
1/2 Teaspoon Pepper
1/2 Cup Water

Directions:
Remove outer husks and the corn silk from the ears of corn. Rinse corn under cold running water. Hold each ear of corn with one hand and use a sharp knife to cut the kernels from the cob scraping the cobs well to remove all milk.

In a heavy skillet (cast iron), melt butter over medium high heat. Mix the corn and any liquid from the corn with the sugar, salt, flour, pepper and water, stirring well. Put corn mixture into the skillet and stir constantly as the mixture will thicken. Cook 10 to 15 minutes over medium heat until tender.

Serves 2 to 4.

Spoon
BREAD

Ingredients:
2 Cups White or Yellow Plain Corn Meal
6 Cups Milk
4 Tablespoons Butter
2 Teaspoons Salt
2 Teaspoons Baking Powder
4 Beaten Eggs

Directions:
Combine meal and milk in top of a double boiler and cook over boiling water about 1/2 hour or to a mushy consistency. Stir in butter, salt, and baking powder. Slowly add beaten eggs, stirring constantly, so the eggs will not "cook" in the hot liquid.

Pour into a 9 by 12 inch pan or 3 quart casserole and bake in a hot oven at 375 degrees about 30 minutes. Serve hot as an accompaniment with the roast and gravy or with the baked chicken.

Serves 8 to 10.

Homemade
VANILLA ICE CREAM

Ingredients:
4 (12 Ounce) Cans Evaporated Milk
8 Cups Half and Half
4 Cups Sugar
1/2 Teaspoon Salt
12 Beaten Eggs
3 Tablespoons Vanilla

Directions:
Mix milk, half and half, sugar, and salt in a large sauce pan. Over medium heat, stir approximately 15 minutes. Slowly add beaten eggs to the hot mixture stirring constantly. *(Hint: Slowly stir a cup of the hot mixture into the eggs first to raise the temperature of the eggs.)* Let cool. Add vanilla.

Freeze in hand cranked or electric freezer following manufacturer's instructions.

Pound CAKE

Ingredients:
1 Box of Confectioner's Sugar
1 Pound Butter (Softened)
6 Eggs
4 Cups Cake Flour (Sift 2 times)
1 Teaspoon Vanilla Extract
1 Teaspoon Lemon Extract

Directions:
Cream together sugar and butter in a large mixing bowl. Add eggs, beating constantly. Add 1 cup of sifted flour, and beat until smooth. Repeat with 1 cup at a time until all 4 cups of flour have been added. Add 1 teaspoon of vanilla extract. Add 1 tablespoon of lemon extract. Mix well.

Pour into a greased and floured pound cake pan or bundt pan. Bake for an hour and 15 minutes at 350 degrees.

Church PICNIC

FRIED CHICKEN

DEVILED EGGS

POTATO SALAD

SWEET POTATO PIE

LEMONADE OR
ORANGEADE

For most of the rural South, and particularly among people of color, traditions were deeply rooted in the church. The Bones attended Springlake Baptist Church. It was there that people joined in the celebrations of life when there were marriages and baptisms. It was also there that people held each other to their hearts in times of grief and loss.

But oh, what a place the church became when the congregation gathered together in the spirit of fun! Only softball, horseshoes, checkers or sack races could lure a person away from a crispy chicken drumstick, a fragrant slice of sweet potato pie or a tall, cool glass of lemonade. Lured away to play...but soon they would come back for more!

Fried CHICKEN

Ingredients:
Desired Chicken Pieces
Salt
Pepper
Seasoned Salt
Paprika
Flour
Peanut Oil

Directions:
Wash pieces of chicken well. Season both sides of chicken with salt, pepper, seasoned salt and paprika to desired taste. Cover both sides of chicken with flour. Shake excess flour off each chicken piece.

Fill a large, heavy skillet about halfway with peanut oil. Heat oil over medium heat so that a pinch of flour dropped into the oil will bubble. Put chicken pieces into the skillet, but do not crowd pieces. Fry chicken uncovered, approximately 15 to 20 minutes depending on the size of the pieces, turning once or twice until golden brown and juices run clear. Remove chicken with tongs and let drain on paper towels.

Deviled

EGGS

Ingredients:
6 Eggs
1/4 Cup of a Top Quality Mayonnaise
2 Teaspoons Sweet Pickle Relish
Salt and Pepper to Taste
Paprika

Directions:
Boil eggs about 5 minutes until hard-boiled. Remove the shells from the eggs. Cut each egg in half lengthwise. Carefully remove yolks.

Mash yolks and mix with mayonnaise and sweet pickle relish. Add salt and pepper to taste. Spoon or pipe yolk mixture into egg white halves. Place on platter. Lightly sprinkle paprika over the yolk mixture. Chill and serve.

Makes a dozen deviled egg halves.

Potato SALAD

Ingredients:
6 Red Potatoes
Salt
White Pepper
3 Chopped Hard Boiled Eggs
2 Tablespoons Chopped Pimento
2 Tablespoons Chopped Onions
1/4 Cup Chopped Sweet Pickle (or Sweet Relish)
2 Tablespoons Chopped Green Pepper
3 Tablespoons Chopped Celery
1 Cup of a Top Quality Mayonnaise
1/4 Teaspoon Sugar

Directions:
In a sauce pan, cover potatoes with water and boil until soft to touch. Drain potatoes, and set aside to cool. When cool, peel potatoes and cube. Season potatoes with salt and pepper to taste. Toss with remaining ingredients. Chill and serve.

(If you prefer a creamier potato salad, add more mayonnaise.)

Serves 6 to 8.

Pie Crust

Ingredients:
2 Cups of Flour
1 Teaspoon Salt
1/4 Tablespoon Sugar
2/3 Cup Shortening
1 Egg (Small)
1/4 Cup Cold Water (Iced)

Directions
Sift dry ingredients together.
Cut shortening into dry
ingredients with a fork.
Add egg and water and mix well.

Place mixture on a lightly floured surface.
Knead briefly and roll to desired shape.
Place dough into the bottom of a pie
pan, and flute edges.
(This is for a one-crust pie.)

Sweet Potato PIE

Ingredients:
4 Sweet Potatoes
1 Stick Butter
1/4 Cup Evaporated Milk
1 Teaspoon Baking Powder
1 Cup Sugar
2 Eggs
1 Teaspoon Cinnamon
1/2 Teaspoon Nutmeg
1 Teaspoon Vanilla
Pie Crust (recipe follows)

Directions:
Boil potatoes in skin until soft to touch. When cool enough to handle, but still warm enough to melt the butter, peel potatoes. Place peeled potatoes in mixing bowl and add butter, evaporated milk, baking powder, sugar, eggs, spices and vanilla. With the electric mixer on low, beat the potato mixture gently until the mixture is creamy. *(You may use a hand beater in place of an electric mixer, if desired.)*

Pour mixture into prepared pie crust. Bake for 30 minutes in a 300 degree oven.

Serves 6 to 8.

Lemonade/ ORANGEADE

Ingredients:

Juice of 4 Lemons or 8 Oranges
1 Cup Sugar (Add More or Less for Taste)
8 Cups Water
(Optional: May Substitute 2 Cups Club Soda and 6 Cups Water)

Directions:

Add the juice, sugar and water together.
Stir until desired flavor is obtained.
Serves 6 to 8.
Hint: The club soda adds effervescence.

Christmas DINNER

DUCK-N-ORANGE
SAUCE

COUNTRY HAM

TOMATO DUMPLINGS

CORNBREAD DRESSING
& GRAVY

SPECKLED BUTTER
BEANS

EGGNOG

COCONUT CAKE

CHESS PIE

A table gently graced by the lace of grandmothers past ... candles standing brightly amidst pieces of cherished silver ... china catching the light from the window's winter sun.

The holidays of years ago never failed to warm the spirit. Food was such an integral part that preparation for the annual feast was made long in advance. Beneva would remember those celebrations and carry those traditions into later years.

44

Duck-n-Orange
SAUCE

Ingredients:

2 Ducks
4 Stalks Celery, Cut into Large Pieces
1 Onion, Cut Into Quarters
1 Apple, Cut Into Quarters

Salt
Pepper
4 Slices Bacon, Uncooked

Directions:

Wash and dry ducks. Stuff each duck with equal amounts of celery, onion, and apple. Salt and pepper duck, place bacon strips over the breast side, and place the ducks in a roasting pan.
Add 2 cups of water. Cover.

Cook at 450 degrees for 1 hour; then lower heat to 350 degrees, uncover and cook for 30 minutes to an hour until done.
Makes 4 to 6 generous servings.

ORANGE SAUCE

Ingredients:

1 Cup Brown Sugar
1 Cup Granulated Sugar
2 Cups Orange Juice
Dash of Salt
1 Teaspoon Orange Rind

Directions:

Combine ingredients and simmer until thickened.
Pour over ducks and serve.

Country HAM

Ingredients:

1 Whole Country Ham   2 Apples
1/2 Box Dark Brown Sugar   2 Oranges

Directions:

Cut off the ends of the ham, or have a butcher remove the ham hock. Place the ham in a large pot, and cover with water. Soak overnight in cold water. Drain water from the ham, and replace with fresh water.

Put 1/2 box of dark brown sugar in the pot holding the ham. Cut up 2 apples and 2 oranges (both unpeeled) and place those pieces in the pot. Bring to a boil and let simmer for 20 minutes per pound. Take the ham out of the pot, and allow to cool. Slice the ham very thin and serve.

Tomato DUMPLINGS

Ingredients:

1 Pound Ground Sausage   2 Cups Flour
2 Cups Tomato Sauce   1/2 Teaspoon Salt
2 Cups Canned Stewed Tomatoes   4 Teaspoons Baking Powder
Salt   3/4 Cup Water
Pepper

Directions:

Form sausage into small cakes. Fry in deep pot until brown. Add tomatoes. Season to taste with salt and pepper. Heat until boiling.

Sift flour, salt, and baking powder. Add water. Beat until smooth. Drop one teaspoon at a time of the flour mixture into the boiling tomato mixture. Cover tightly. Boil for 10 minutes. Serves 6 to 8.

Cornbread
DRESSING

Dressing Ingredients:

8 Cups Cornbread
1 Chopped Yellow Onion
1 Diced Bell Pepper
4 Stalks Celery
1 Stick Butter, Melted
4 Slices of White Bread, Toasted

4 Eggs, Beaten
1 Tablespoon Sage
Salt and Pepper to Taste
4 Cups Chicken Broth
(may use canned)

Directions for Dressing:

In a skillet or pan, sauté onion, bell pepper, and celery in the butter. Pour the butter and vegetable mixture into the bowl of crumbled cornbread. Crumble the toasted white bread and add to the bowl. Add beaten eggs, sage, salt and pepper, mixing thoroughly. Pour in the chicken broth and mix well. Pour into 10 x 13 inch lightly-greased pan or baking dish and bake at 400 degrees until done. Dressing will brown slightly on the top and feel somewhat firm to the touch. Makes 6 to 8 servings.

CORNBREAD

1 1/2 Cups Self-Rising White Corn Meal
1 Egg
3/4 Cup Buttermilk
1 Teaspoon Sugar

Pinch of Salt
Pinch of Soda
1/2 Stick Melted Butter

Combine all ingredients and place in a greased black skillet. Bake in preheated oven at 350 degrees about 20 minutes or until browned. When cooled, crumble and reserve for dressing.

Speckled
BUTTER BEANS

Ingredients:
2 Cups Shelled, Fresh, Speckled Butter Beans or
1 Box Frozen Beans
Water, Covering 2 Inches Over Beans
1 Teaspoon Salt
1 to 2 Tablespoons Butter or Oil
Salt and Pepper

Directions:
For fresh beans, rinse and inspect beans carefully. Discard any that
are ruined or discolored.

Bring water and salt to a boil. Add butter or oil. Add beans.
Cook about 20 to 30 minutes or until tender. Season to taste.
*(If you prefer, a small piece of smoked ham may be added to the cooking
water before putting in the beans.)*
Makes 4 servings.

Egg
NOG

Ingredients:
4 Eggs, Separated
4 Tablespoons of Sugar
2 Cups Milk
2 Cups Half & Half
1/4 Teaspoon Salt
1 Teaspoon Vanilla
1/2 Cup Brandy or Bourbon of your choice (optional)
1 Cup Whipping Cream
Nutmeg

Directions:
Beat 4 egg yolks; add sugar, milk, half and half, and salt, beating well. Add vanilla. The mixture should have a smooth pale yellow consistency and should easily coat a spoon. Refrigerate.

Before serving, beat 4 egg whites until stiff. Beat the whipping cream until stiff. If desired, add the brandy or bourbon to the egg yolk mixture, then fold in the stiff egg whites. Fill cups with the eggnog and garnish with whipped cream and a sprinkle of nutmeg.
Makes 4 to 6 cups.

Coconut CAKE

PINEAPPLE FILLING
Ingredients:
1 Can Crushed Pineapple
1 Tablespoon Flour
1 Tablespoon Butter
Grated Rind of 1 Orange
Juice From 1 Orange

Directions:
Combine all ingredients over medium heat. Stirring occasionally, lower heat and simmer until thickened and set aside.

BASIC CAKE
Ingredients:

3 Sticks Butter
2 Cups Sugar
1 Tablespoon Vegetable Shortening
4 Eggs
3 Cups Cake Flour

2 Teaspoons Baking Powder
1 Cup Milk
3 Teaspoons Vanilla Extract
1 Teaspoon Lemon Extract

Directions:
Cream butter, sugar, and shortening. Add eggs one at a time until all 4 are added. Sift together flour and baking powder. Add egg mixture to flour mixture, alternating several times until combined. Add milk to flour and egg mixture, also alternating several times until combined. Add vanilla and lemon extracts.

CONTINUED

Place mixture in two 10 inch or three 9 inch pans.
Bake for 30 minutes at 350 degrees.
*(Place toothpick in middle of cake. If toothpick comes
up clean, the cake is done.)* Let layers cool.

WHITE ICING
Ingredients:

1 Chilled Egg White	1 Teaspoon Vanilla
1 Cup Sugar	1 Bag Frozen Coconut
1/2 Cup Boiling Water	1 Can Shredded Coconut
1/4 Teaspoon Cream of Tartar	

Directions:

Beat egg white and sugar in a high speed mixer. Add boiling water
slowly in order to keep the water from splattering. Add cream of
tartar and vanilla. Beat until peaks hold their shape. Mix frozen and
shredded coconut together. Set aside.

COCONUT CAKE ASSEMBLY
Directions:

For two layers:
1. Ice bottom layer.
2. Spread pineapple filling over the bottom layer's icing
and sprinkle a small amount of coconut on top.
3. Place the second layer on top, ice top and sides, and sprinkle
remaining coconut generously over tops and sides.

For three layers, repeat step 2 for the second layer.
Place the third layer on top, ice top and sides and
sprinkle remaining coconut generously over tops and sides.

Chess
PIE

Ingredients:
1 Stick Butter
1 1/2 Cups Sugar
3 Eggs, Lightly Beaten
2 Tablespoons Buttermilk
1 1/2 Teaspoons White Vinegar
1 Teaspoon Vanilla
1 1/2 Teaspoon Plain Corn Meal
Prepared Pie Crust

Directions:
Melt butter and stir in sugar. Add eggs, buttermilk, vinegar, vanilla, and meal. Mix well. Pour into pie crust *(see crust recipe for Sweet Potato Pie on page 42)* and bake at 425 degrees for 10 minutes. Reduce heat to 350 degrees. Cook for 30 minutes or until it is brown and shakes slightly. Let the pie cool and set before serving.

What southern family does not have its very own New Year's Day traditions? Church at midnight and "watch meetings" bringing in the New Year were common in young Beneva's time.

Also common were the customs of cleaning the house from top to bottom, and being very careful about the first person to enter the house on New Year's Day! (An old belief, particularly among African-Americans in the South, was that allowing a man to enter first brought good luck to the home.)

Without a doubt, though, it is the tradition of eating certain foods on New Year's Day that remains a regional and cultural legacy. The cooking of greens, black-eyed peas, and other foods at the beginning of the year evolves from the belief that they will bring prosperity and good luck.

We say "Let the tradition continue!"

53

New Year's Day
DINNER

CHITTERLINGS

PIG FEET

BLACK-EYED PEAS

BAKED SWEET POTATOES

COLLARD GREENS

BOILED OKRA

FRIED PIES

Chitterlings

Ingredients:

10 Pounds Chitterlings (available in most grocery stores)*
1 Medium Chopped Onion
1 Teaspoon Crushed Red Pepper or 1 Whole Red Pepper
2 Teaspoons Salt
1/2 Teaspoon Ground Black Pepper
2 Cups Water
1 Potato
Defrost chitterlings in refrigerator overnight.

Directions:

Wash the chitterlings with warm water, and clean thoroughly of all debris. Using a small knife, cut away as much of the fat lining as possible. *(This may take an hour or more to complete.)*
Rinse the chitterlings with cold water, and drain.

Place the chitterlings in a medium pot. Add onions and seasonings. Add 1 cup of water. Scrub the potato, slice in half, and add it to the pot. (The potato will help absorb the chitterlings' intense aroma.) Bring the chitterlings to a boil. Cover and reduce the heat to very low. Simmer the chitterlings for 3 hours or until tender. Add more water if needed.

Remove the potato and discard. Serve the chitterlings hot.
Serves 2 to 3.

Pig
FEET

Ingredients:

Pig Feet *(found packaged in the meat sections of grocery stores)*
Water
Red Pepper Pods or Cracked Red Pepper
Salt
Pepper
One Tablespoon Vinegar

Directions:

Wash the pig feet thoroughly. Place in a pot and add water to cover. Bring the water to a high boil. The water will cloud, especially around the top. Skim this part off. Add the salt, pepper and red pepper and bring to a boil. Lower heat and let simmer for an hour or more until meat is tender. Add one teaspoon of vinegar to the pot for taste.

Hint: For each serving, purchase two pig feet as packaged.

Black Eyed PEAS

Ingredients:
1 Pound Dried Black Eyed Peas
1 Ham Hock or 1 Piece Salt Pork (About 4 Ounces)
Salt
Pepper
1/4 Teaspoon Sugar

Directions:
Sort peas; removing discolored peas. Wash and cover with cold water and soak overnight. Drain water from peas.

Cover ham hock with water and boil for one hour before adding peas. Add peas to ham hock. Cover and simmer for 30 minutes or until desired tenderness. Season with salt, pepper, and sugar to taste. Serves 4 to 6.

Boiled
OKRA

Ingredients:

1 Pound of Fresh Okra
Salt
Pepper
Butter

Directions:

Wash okra, and cut off the stems. Make sure okra pods are not too large, as they will be tough. Cover okra with water in a pot, and bring to a boil. Cook covered for 5 to 10 minutes or until tender.

Add salt, pepper, and butter to taste. Serve hot.

Baked SWEET POTATOES

Ingredients:

Medium Sweet Potatoes *(I Potato per Person)*
Butter

Directions:

Rub potatoes clean under running water. Wipe dry. Place potatoes in a preheated oven at 400 degrees. Bake for 30 to 40 minutes or until soft. Serve with butter.

Hint: Rub potatoes all over with a very small amount of vegetable oil before baking. Lightly piercing the potato once with the tines of a fork also helps in the baking process.

Collard GREENS

Ingredients:

2 Large Bunches of Collard Greens

1 Piece of Salt Pork (About 4 Ounces)

Salt

Pepper

Pinch of Sugar

1 Red Pepper (or 1/2 Teaspoon Crushed Red Pepper)

Directions:

Pick and remove stems from greens. Wash greens thoroughly. Break up large leaves into pieces. Boil salt pork in 6 to 8 cups of water for approximately 30 minutes. Add greens and bring to a boil. Lower heat and cook for approximately one to two hours or until tender. *(Collards take longer to cook than turnip greens.)* Add a pinch of sugar and the red pepper. If a pepper pod is used, remove before serving. Serves 4 to 6.

Fried
PIES

Ingredients:

1 Cup Sugar

1 (10 Ounce) Package of Dried Peaches
or Apples, Chopped

2 Cups Water

1/2 Cup (One Stick) Butter

1 1/2 Teaspoon Lemon Juice

1 Teaspoon Cinnamon

1/2 Teaspoon Almond Extract

Cooking Oil

Directions:

Put the dried chopped peaches (or apples), water and sugar in a large saucepan and bring to a boil over medium heat. While the fruit is simmering, prepare the pastry Reduce heat to low and simmer for an hour and a half or until the fruit is tender. Add the butter, lemon juice, cinnamon and almond extract. Mash the mixture together thoroughly and let cool for thirty minutes.

PASTRY INGREDIENTS:

2 Cups Sifted All Purpose Flour

1 Teaspoon Saltr

1/2 Cup Shortening

1/3 Cup Cold Water

Sift together the flour and salt. Cut in shortening with a fork until the dough resembles peas in size. Add the cold water and mix well. Roll into a ball and chill for 30 minutes. When ready to prepare the crust, roll dough out into 6-inch rounds. Place cooled fruit filling on one half of the dough and fold the other half over, forming a crescent shaped pie. Seal edges with water and crimp with a fork.

Pour a quarter of an inch of oil in a large skillet and heat. When ready to fry, put two pies in the skillet at a time and brown on both sides. Remove from skillet and drain on paper towels.

AT *Home* ON PROVINE STREET

THE CHILD REARING YEARS

One bright Sunday in 1948, Springlake Baptist Church found itself missing two young members from its pews. Beneva had left services early to join Twillard Mayweather, a spirited young man who lived nearby, for a Sunday ride. The family knew Beneva left with Twillard and thought nothing of it, assuming she would return as she always did.

But this time, it was different.

Like most young mothers, Beneva wanted to provide a variety of meals for her husband and children, while carving out time for work, activities and special occasions.

The two had known each other for a number of years, and Twillard had returned to his Arkansas home following his military duty in World War II. According to her youngest sister Anna, the family had become accustomed to seeing him since he came by often to visit Beneva, sometimes riding his favorite horse, Dan. Twillard, with his military experience and a good head for business, had accepted a lucrative job with a noted Arkansas entrepreneur. They obviously felt the time was right for them to marry - so they did. And they told no one.

As eldest sister Ella tells the story, when they returned, Beneva was afraid to tell her parents, so she tried to persuade Ella to break the news. "I really believe Beneva just didn't want to cut any more spinach," Ella laughs, but the family couldn't have been more comfortable with the union. They knew it would result in a lifelong partnership.

The couple moved to Marianna, Arkansas where they began married life. Daughter Emma was born there before another job change for Twillard took them to Detroit. There, a second daughter, Patricia, was born. After staying there for a few years, the family moved back to the South and settled in Memphis. For a time, Beneva enjoyed her years at home, caring for her growing family. Later, she worked at William Terrell Hospital, a well known medical facility in Memphis.

By this time, daughters Eva and Cynthia were born and the needs of the family had changed. Like most young mothers, Beneva wanted to provide a variety of meals for her husband and children, while carving out time for work, activities and special occasions. Many of her meals mirrored those of most young mothers at that time - simple and quick, yet wholesome. For special occasions, though, she'd pull out the stops!

Heaven & Hell
PARTY

HOT CHOCOLATE

CHILI

DEVIL'S FOOD CAKE

AMBROSIA

HEAVENLY SALAD

ANGEL DELIGHT

A good Heaven & Hell party was legendary during the '50s and '60s. For some it was potluck; for others it was catered to the max! Foods ranged from the hottest dishes such as spicy chili or soups, to the coolest dishes such as ice cream and sherbet. Or, as this menu suggests, it spotlighted foods with heavenly names such as Angel Delight and Ambrosia to foods with - well, you can take it from there...

Hot
CHOCOLATE

Ingredients:
2 1/2 Cups Milk, Scalded
2 Ounces (Two Squares) Unsweetened Chocolate, Quartered
1/4 Cup Sugar
1 Teaspoon Vanilla Extract
Dash Salt

Directions:
Rinse an electric blender container with hot water. Pour into the warmed container about a half cup of scalded milk. Add chocolate, sugar, vanilla extract and salt. Cover and blend about one minute or until smooth and color is even throughout.

Uncover and add remaining scalded milk. Blend until thoroughly mixed. Serve immediately. Makes 2 cups.

Chili

Ingredients:
1 Large Onion, Chopped
1 Green Pepper, Chopped
1 Tablespoon Vegetable Oil
2 Pounds Ground Beef
2 Cups Vegetable Juice
1 (1.3 Ounce) Can Chili Powder
1 (10 Ounce) Can Hot, Diced Tomatoes
1 (15 Ounce) Can Stewed Tomatoes
3 Bay Leaves
1/2 Teaspoon Sugar
1 Teaspoon Salt
Dash Pepper
1 (16 Ounce) Can Kidney Beans, Drained and Rinsed

Directions:
In a large skillet or Dutch oven, sauté onion and bell pepper in oil until tender. Add ground beef; brown, crumble, and drain.

Add all other ingredients to the beef mixture except the kidney beans. Stir well. Bring to a boil, reduce heat, and simmer uncovered for 45 minutes to 1 hour. Add beans the last 15 minutes. Remove the bay leaves when done. Makes 6 generous servings.

Devil's Food CAKE

Ingredients:

2 Cups Sifted Cake Flour
2 Tablespoons Baking Powder
1/4 Teaspoon Baking Soda
1/2 Teaspoon Salt
2/3 Cup Butter, Softened
1 2/3 Cup Sugar
3 Eggs, Beaten
3 Squares Unsweetened Baking Chocolate, Melted
1 Cup Milk
1 Teaspoon Vanilla

Directions:

In a bowl, combine sifted flour, baking powder, baking soda, and salt. In a separate bowl, cream butter, and gradually add sugar until the mixture is light and fluffy. Add eggs and beat well; then gradually add cooled melted chocolate. Add in the flour mixture alternating with milk. Beat after each addition until smooth. Add in vanilla and blend. Pour into 2 nine-inch greased layer baking pans.
Bake at 350 degrees for 25 minutes.

CHOCOLATE FROSTING

Ingredients:

4 Squares Unsweetened Chocolate
1 Stick Butter
4 Cups Powdered Sugar
Half and Half Cream
1 Teaspoon Vanilla

Directions:

Melt Chocolate and butter. Let cool. In a mixing bowl, combine chocolate mixture and sugar. Add half and half until desired spreading consistency is reached. Add vanilla and spread over cake.

Ambrosia

Ingredients:

9 Oranges, Peeled, Seeded, and Sectioned
2 (20 Ounce) Cans of Crushed Pineapple, Drained
1 Cup of Honey
1 to 2 Teaspoons of Almond Extract
1 Cup of Flaked Coconut

Directions:

Combine all ingredients in a glass bowl. Cover mixture and chill at least 8 hours. Serves 8 to 10.

Heavenly SALAD

Ingredients:

3 Ounce Package Peach Gelatin
1 Cup Boiling Water
1 (8 Ounce) Package Cream Cheese, Softened
1 Cup Pecans
1 (8 Ounce) Can Crushed Pineapple, Undrained
1 Teaspoon Vanilla
1 Cup Peach Flavored Soda

Directions:

Combine all ingredients, adding peach flavored soda last. Pour into salad mold or casserole dish and chill until set. Remove from mold and decorate on a bed of lettuce, or spoon and serve on individual dishes.

Angel DELIGHT

Ingredients:

1 Purchased Sponge Cake
3 Tablespoons Sherry
2 Cups of Vanilla Custard
1/2 Cup Confectioners' Sugar
1 Quart of Whipping Cream
Beneva's Chocolate Sauce*
(see "Elegant Entertaining/Debutante Night" for Recipe on page 141)

Directions:

Cut off top half of cake. Sprinkle the bottom half with sherry before spreading with boiled custard. Place the other half on top. Add 1/2 cup confectioners' sugar to whipping cream. Beat cream until stiff. Ice with whipped cream and drizzle with chocolate sauce.

BOILED CUSTARD

Ingredients:

1/2 Cup Sugar
1 1/2 Teaspoons All-Purpose Flour
2 Eggs, Well Beaten
2 Cups Milk, Scalded
1 Teaspoon Vanilla

Directions:

In saucepan, mix sugar with flour and add eggs, beating well. Gradually add hot milk, stirring until blended. Pour into double boiler and cook until mixture coats spoon, stirring constantly. Add vanilla. Remove from heat and let cool.

After Prom PARTY

HOT SAUSAGE & EGG CASSEROLE

CHEESE RICE

FRENCH TOAST

BLUEBERRY MUFFINS

BANANA NUT BREAD

A LESSON IN MULTIPLICATION:
Junior and Senior Proms X Four Daughters = One Busy Mom!

The math says it all! Luckily for Beneva, an additional talent for sewing came in pretty handy during those days.

Prom night is a special event in a young person's life and its place in the high school experience ranks high. The dress, the corsage, Dad's newly polished car... they all add up to an equation with the total sum of fun!

And what could better top off prom night than an early breakfast (a late, light supper?) complete with French Toast or Muffins and a tasty breakfast casserole! Prom Perfect!

Hot Sausage
& EGG CASSEROLE

Ingredients:

8 Slices White Bread
2 Pounds Hot Sausage
12 Eggs, Beaten
2 Cups Half & Half
1 Teaspoon Dry Mustard
1/2 Pound Sharp Cheddar Cheese, Grated

Directions:

Butter a 3 quart casserole. Trim crust from bread before lining the bottom of the casserole dish with the bread.

Brown the sausage and drain. Combine eggs, sausage, half & half, and dry mustard in a large mixing bowl. Stir in half the cheese. Pour into a casserole dish. Sprinkle top with the remainder of the cheese. Cover and refrigerate overnight.

Preheat oven to 300 degrees. Bake for an hour and fifteen minutes or until mixture is firm. Serves 6 to 8.

Cheese RICE

Ingredients:
Hot, Cooked Rice
1/2 Stick Butter
1 Cup Cheddar Cheese, Grated

Directions:
Follow package directions for the desired servings of rice. For 4 to 6 servings of fully cooked rice, add 1/2 stick of butter and 1 cup of grated cheese. Taste and make adjustments as needed.

French TOAST

Ingredients:
4 Slices Texas Bread (Thick Cut)
6 Eggs
1 Cup Half & Half

2 to 4 Tablespoons Cinnamon
Confectioner's Sugar (Optional)
Buttered Syrup

Directions:
Beat eggs, half & half, and cinnamon in bowl. Dip each slice of bread into mixture before placing on lightly-oiled hot griddle. If frying in a skillet, pre-pare skillet by heating 1/2 tablespoon of butter and 1/2 tablespoon of oil.

Cook on griddle or in hot oiled skillet, turning bread after browning on one side. Cook on both sides.

If desired, sprinkle additional cinnamon on toast before turning. Confectioner's sugar may be sprinkled on toast after toast is cooked. Pour hot buttered syrup over toast. *(For hot buttered syrup, stir together 1 cup of your favorite syrup with 2 tablespoons of butter. Microwave until warm.)*

Blueberry MUFFINS

Ingredients:
1 Cup Sugar
1/2 Cup Butter, Softened
2 Eggs
1/2 Cup Milk
2 Cups All-Purpose Flour
2 Teaspoons Baking Powder
1/2 Teaspoon Salt
2 Cups Fresh or Frozen Blueberries
*(If blueberries are frozen, allow them to thaw,
then rinse before using.)*

Directions:
Combine sugar, butter, eggs and milk in a mixing bowl;
beat well. Combine flour, baking powder and salt. Add
to egg mixture and mix until blended. Fold in blueberries.

Spoon into 12 well-greased muffin cups filling the cups
almost to the top. Bake at 375 degrees for 20 to 25
minutes. Remove from pans to cool.

Banana Nut
BREAD

Ingredients:
1 Stick Butter, Softened
11/2 Cups Sugar
2 Eggs
3 Large Bananas, Mashed
3 Cups All-Purpose Flour
1/2 Teaspoon Baking Soda
1/2 Teaspoon Salt
1/2 Cup Chopped Pecans

Directions:
Preheat oven to 300 degrees. Blend butter, sugar, and eggs in a bowl. Add mashed bananas. Add flour, baking soda, and salt. Mix very well. Blend in pecans.

Pour into 2 greased, floured loaf pans. Bake for 40 to 45 minutes at 300 degrees.

PTA meetings, dance classes, doctors' appointments – the list goes on and on. The demands of a growing family place a strain on the most resilient parent. Having grown up in a large family, Beneva was accustomed to preparing meals that were satisfying yet easy on the cook. These dishes were staples in our home and we enjoy them even today.

Family
DINNER
Quick and Easy

MEAT LOAF

MACARONI AND
CHEESE CASSEROLE

GREEN PEAS

CORNBREAD MUFFINS

BANANA PUDDING

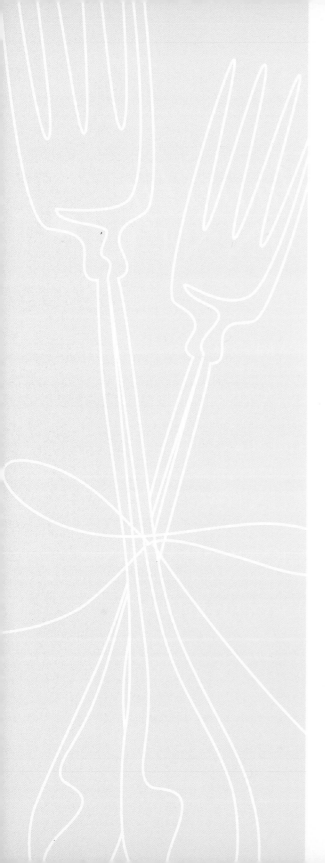

Meat
LOAF

Ingredients:
2 Pounds Ground Beef
1 Egg, Slightly Beaten
1 Small Onion, Chopped
1 Cup Cracker Crumbs
2 Teaspoons Salt
2 Teaspoons Pepper
1 (6 ounce) Can Tomato Paste

Directions:
Combine all ingredients. Mix and blend well. Form into loaf or roll.
Place into loaf pan or shallow baking pan. Preheat oven to 350 degrees.
Bake for 1/2 hour; then pour tomato sauce glaze over loaf. Continue
baking at the same temperature for another 1/2 hour or until done.
Makes 4 to 6 generous servings.

MEAT LOAF TOMATO GLAZE

Ingredients:
3 Cups Ketchup
1 Cup Dark Brown Sugar
2 Tablespoons Yellow Mustard

Directions:
Combine ingredients and mix well. Pour glaze over meatloaf.

Macaroni & Cheese
CASSEROLE

Ingredients:

(1/2) 16 ounce Bag Macaroni	2 Tablespoons Chopped Green Onions
Salt	2 Tablespoons Chopped Pimentos
White Pepper	Cheese Sauce (recipe follows)
	1 Cup Sharp Cheddar Cheese, Grated

Directions:

Cook macaroni to package specifications. Drain, rinse, and pour into casserole dish. Season the macaroni with salt and white pepper. Add chopped green onions and chopped pimentos.

Pour cheese sauce over cooked macaroni. Mix well. Cover top of casserole with grated sharp cheddar cheese.

Bake in the oven at 350 degrees for 30 to 40 minutes until well heated and cheese melts. Makes 4 to 6 servings.

CHEESE CREAM SAUCE

Ingredients:

4 Tablespoons Butter	2 Cups Half & Half
4 Tablespoons Flour	1 Cup Sharp Cheddar Cheese
1 Teaspoon Salt	

Directions:

Mix ingredients over medium heat stirring constantly until mixture thickens.

Green PEAS

Ingredients:
1 Package Frozen Green Peas
Salt
Pepper
1/2 Stick Butter

Directions:
Bring 1/4 cup of water to a boil. Add green peas and cover. When peas are cooked, add 1/2 stick of butter, and salt and pepper to taste. Serves 4.

Cornbread MUFFINS

Ingredients:

2 Cups Yellow Corn Meal
1/2 Cup Flour
1 Teaspoon Baking Powder
1/2 Teaspoon Baking Soda
1/2 Teaspoon Salt

2 Teaspoons Sugar
2 Eggs
2 Cups Buttermilk
1/4 Cup (1/2 Stick) Melted Butter

Directions:
In a large bowl, combine dry ingredients. Add eggs and buttermilk and stir until blended. Stir in melted butter. Pour into greased muffin tins and fill about two-thirds full. Bake at 375 degrees for about 20 minutes or until tops are golden. Let set for a few minutes before removing.

Banana PUDDING

Ingredients:

3 1/2 Tablespoons Flour
1 1/3 Cups Sugar
3 Egg Yolks
1 Cup Half & Half
2 Cups Milk

Pinch of Salt
1 Teaspoon Vanilla
1 (12 ounce) Box Vanilla Wafers
6 Medium Bananas
Meringue Topping (recipe follows)

Directions:

Combine flour, sugar, egg yolks, half & half, milk and salt in a heavy saucepan. Cook over medium heat, stirring constantly until mixture is smooth and thick. Remove from heat and stir in the vanilla.

Line the bottom and sides of a 3 quart pan or dish with vanilla wafers. Slice bananas and lay over vanilla wafers. Pour 1/3 of custard mixture over bananas. Repeat layers.

Spread meringue topping over pudding. Bake at 425 degrees for 10 minutes or until top is golden brown.

MERINGUE TOPPING

Ingredients:

3 Egg Whites
1/4 Cup + 2 Tablespoons Sugar
1 Teaspoon Vanilla

Directions:

Beat egg whites until stiff. Gradually add all of sugar beating until stiff peaks form. Add in vanilla and blend well. Spread meringue over pudding. Bake at 425 degrees for 10 minutes or until top is golden brown. Serves 4 to 6.

Thanksgiving
DINNER

TURKEY

OYSTER DRESSING

SWEET POTATO CASSEROLE

GREEN BEAN CASSEROLE

SPINACH

SWEET POTATO PIE

PECAN PIE

SPICED TEA

With all of our Mother's expertise in creating beautiful, complex dishes, the table in the Mayweather home at Thanksgiving seemed to reflect the simplicity of her upbringing. For us, like for others, the turkey was the centerpiece of the meal and the side dishes were those we all know and love.

Even now, southern holidays are not complete without sweet potatoes! No southerner alive can deny that this starchy tuber is best presented mashed and buttered in a casserole, or spiced with cinnamon, nutmeg and sugar and baked in a crust.

Neither is a holiday complete without Southern pecans! Floating on top of a rich, sweet pie flavored with dark syrup and vanilla, their crunchy texture reminds us of the wonderful treats that autumn brings.

Turkey

Ingredients:
(1) 10 - 12 Pound Turkey
1 Stick Butter
Salt
Pepper
2 Stalks Celery, Washed
1 Onion
2 Cups Water

Directions:
Wash and remove giblets. Place turkey breast side up in roasting pan. Rub softened butter over turkey breast, and sprinkle with salt and pepper. Place cut up celery, onion, and water in roaster. Cover with foil and bake at 350 degrees for approximately 2 hours (check cooking time per pound on the wrapper for accuracy). Baste often. Uncover and bake for 15 more minutes to brown.

Test doneness by inserting a sharp knife into the thigh of the turkey. If juice runs clear without any trace of blood and the bone wiggles in the socket, the turkey is done. Many turkeys now sold have "pop-up" thermometers that also indicate when the turkey is done.

OYSTER DRESSING

Ingredients:
✢ For Dressing Recipe, see menu for Cornbread Dressing in the "Down Home / Christmas Dinner" section of this book on page 47.
✢ 1 Quart Oysters (Fresh or Frozen)

Directions:
Drain oysters. Cook in a skillet over medium heat (no oil) for 5 to 6 minutes. Drain again and chop. Stir cooked and chopped oysters into dressing before baking.

Sweet Potato
CASSEROLE

Ingredients:

4 Large Sweet Potatoes	2 Eggs
1/2 Cup Butter (1 Stick)	1/4 Teaspoon Nutmeg
1 Cup Sugar	1/2 Teaspoon Cinnamon

Directions:

Boil Potatoes. Peel and place potatoes in a mixing bowl. Add butter, sugar, and eggs. Beat well. Add nutmeg and cinnamon to mixture. Pour into casserole dish. Top with brown sugar topping (see below) or top with marshmallows. Bake for 15 to 20 minutes at 350 degrees.

BROWN SUGAR TOPPING

Ingredients:

1/2 Cup Brown Sugar
1/2 Cup Pecans, Chopped
1 Cup Corn Flakes, Crushed

Combine all ingredients and mix well. Use for topping on the sweet potato casserole.

MARSHMALLOW TOPPING

1 Bag Miniature Marshmallows

Place marshmallows on the casserole after it has heated thoroughly. Return to the oven for another 5 or 10 minutes until marshmallows have browned slightly. Remove from the oven to prevent the marshmallows from burning.

Green Bean CASSEROLE

Ingredients:

3 (9 Ounce) Packages Frozen, French-Style Green Beans
1 (10 3/4 Ounce) Can Cream of Mushroom Soup, Undiluted
1 (8 Ounce) Can Sliced Water Chestnuts, Drained
1 Minced Garlic Clove
2 Tablespoons Finely-Chopped Onions
1/4 Teaspoon Pepper
1 1/2 Cups (6 Ounce) Shredded Cheddar Cheese
1 (2 Ounce) Package Slivered Almonds, Lightly Toasted

Directions:

Thaw green beans; drain. In a saucepan, heat soup; stir in green beans, water chestnuts, garlic, onion, pepper, and cheese.
Turn off heat.

Spoon mixture into a lightly greased 2-quart casserole; top with almonds. Bake uncovered at 375 degrees for 30 minutes.
Makes 4 to 6 servings.

Spinach

Ingredients:
2 Pounds Fresh Spinach
2 Tablespoons Butter
Salt
Pepper

Directions:
Remove the stems and wash spinach in cold water. Repeat several times until clean.

In a large saucepan, bring 2 cups of water to a boil. Drop spinach into the pan and continue to cook on high for about 5 minutes. Spinach cooks quickly and needs very little water. Season with butter, salt and pepper. Serves 4 to 6.

Variations: In the South, some cooks served the spinach with "extras."
Suggestions: Sliced, hard–boiled eggs or grated onions.

SWEET POTATO PIE
See "Down Home/Church Picnic" Section page 42 for the Recipe.

Pecan PIE

Ingredients:

3 Large Eggs	1 Cup Brown Sugar
1 Cup Dark Syrup	3 Tablespoons Melted Butter, Cooledl
1 Teaspoon Vanilla	Cup Chopped Pecans
1/4 Teaspoon Salt	1 9-inch Pie Shell

Directions:

Preheat oven to 350 degrees. Place all ingredients into a mixing bowl. Beat with a mixer on medium speed until well blended. Pour mixture into the 9-inch pie shell. Decorate the top with pecans. Bake for 50 to 60 minutes or until firm.

PIE CRUST:

Ingredients:

2 Cups of Flour	1 Cup Shortening
1 Teaspoon Salt	1 Egg (Small)
1/4 Tablespoon Sugar	1/4 Cup Cold Water (Iced)

Directions:

Sift dry ingredients together. Cut shortening into dry ingredients with a fork. Add egg and water and mix well.

Place mixture on a lightly floured surface. Knead briefly and roll to desired shape. Place dough into the bottom of a pie pan, and flute edges. (This is a one-crust pie.)

Spiced TEA

Ingredients:
8 Cups Boiling Water
5 Tea Bags
8 Cups Cold Water
1 Teaspoon Whole Cloves
2 Cups Sugar
Juice of 3 Lemons
Juice of 6 Oranges

Directions:
Add boiling water to tea bags. Let stand for 5 minutes. Remove tea bags and cloves. Make a syrup by boiling 8 cups of water, cloves and sugar. Add syrup and fruit juice to tea. Allow to cool. Serve over ice. Makes a little more than a gallon.

Let's do the math again. Four daughters times eighteen years before college times tons of family and friends. Birthdays?

A piece of cake.

Well, several pieces of cake, actually...

Birthdays around the Mayweather home seemed to attract young people. Beneva made sure that each year's celebration was a celebration of life, and with that came fun and good food. Her zest for living was equaled only by that of her children, so what a fun time it was!!

Birthday
PARTY

MINIATURE HAMBURGERS WITH BUNS

CHEESE STRAWS

LITTLE DRUMMIES

BIRTHDAY CAKE

FRUIT PUNCH

Mini Hamburgers
AND BUNS

Ingredients:
1 to 2 Pounds Ground Beef
Salt
Pepper

Directions:

Season ground beef to taste. Shape burgers to fit buns (which can be mde in advance). Bake or fry burgers.

MINI BUNS

Ingredients:

1 Tablespoon Dry Yeast
1/2 Cup Warm Water
1 1/2 Cup Scalded Milk, Cooled to Lukewarm Temperature
1/2 Cup Sugar

2 Teaspoons Salt
3 Eggs, Well-Beaten
1/4 Cup Vegetable Shortening
7 Cups Flour

Directions:

Dissolve yeast in water. Stir in milk, sugar, salt, eggs, shortening. Add half the flour. Mix well. Add remaining flour and mix until smooth. Turn onto floured board and knead 5 to 6 times. Place in greased bowl, cover with a towel, and let dough rise in a warm place until doubled. Roll out and cut with desired cutter.

Place dough circles on a greased baking sheet; set on a stove top to rise for about 15 minutes. Bake in a 400 degree oven until the rolls are light brown (buns cook fast, approximately 10-15 minutes). Extra buns may be frozen.
Makes about 4 to 5 dozen depending on cutter size.

Hint: Make sure water is neither too warm nor too cool, as the wrong temperature will have an adverse effect on the yeast.

Cheese
STRAWS

Ingredients:
1 Cup All-Purpose Flour
1/2 Cup Butter, Softened
2 Cups Extra Sharp, Shredded Cheddar Cheese
1/2 Teaspoon Red Pepper
1/2 Teaspoon Baking Powder

Directions:
Sift flour before measuring. Mash butter in bowl. Add cheese
and remaining ingredients and knead until mixture is smooth
and can be shaped into a ball.

On floured wax paper, roll dough into 1/4 inch thick rectangles.
With a knife cut dough into strips, 3 to 4 inches long. Place on
greased baking sheet. Bake at 350 degrees for about 8 minutes or
until lightly browned. Let cool. Makes 2 dozen.

Little
DRUMMIES

Ingredients:

1 (5 Pound) Bag Chicken Drummies
3 Cups Flour
Salt

Pepper
Seasoned Salt
Cooking Oil

Directions:

Wash drummies. Drain and pat dry. Lightly season drummies with salt, pepper, and seasoned salt. Flour chicken on both sides. Fill pot with cooking oil to 1/2 full. Fry chicken in hot oil 8 to 10 minutes.

Birthday CAKE

Ingredients:

Basic Cake (See "Down Home / Christmas" Section of the Book on page 50.)

BUTTER CREAM ICING FOR BASIC CAKE
1 Cup Butter
1/2 Cup Vegetable Shortening
4 Cups Confectioners' Sugar
1/2 Cup Half & Half
1 Teaspoon Vanilla

Directions:

In mixer, cream all ingredients at medium speed for 2 to 3 minutes. Spread over cake.

Fruit PUNCH

Ingredients:

Simple Syrup (recipe follows)
1 Cup Lemon Juice (Fresh or Concentrated)
1 Can Pineapple Juice
3 Tablespoons Vanilla Extract
3 Tablespoons Almond Extract
Ginger Ale

Directions:

Mix all ingredients except ginger ale in large plastic jug or cooler. Add simple syrup and stir to mix well. Pour over ice. Add ginger ale to taste when serving. Makes about a half gallon.

SIMPLE SYRUP

Ingredients:

4 Cups Sugar
4 Cups Water

Directions:

In a saucepan, bring water and sugar to a boil. Cool and set aside.

Fourth of JULY

BBQ RIBS

BBQ BAKED BEANS

POTATO SALAD

COLESLAW

DEVILED EGGS

PEACH COBBLER

LIMEADE

PEACH ICE CREAM

Reminiscent of childhood days in Arkansas, America's birthday celebration at the Mayweather home consisted of picnic items - baked beans, deviled eggs, potato salad. And in the South, barbeque meant ribs - juicy, succulent pork ribs, smoked over a hot, hickory-spiced fire and basted until perfect. No firecracker could rival the excitement "cleaning off a rib bone" could evoke, and no dip in a pool could cool off a 95   day like a generous scoop of homemade peach ice cream.

Let the festivities begin. . .

Barbeque RIBS

Ingredients:
3 Slabs Pork Loin Back Ribs or Baby Back Ribs
Barbeque Sauce for the Backyard (recipe follows)

Directions:
Marinate ribs overnight in your favorite marinade.

If barbecuing on the grill, make certain the coals are hot. Cook on an oil-coated rack turning once every 15 to 20 minutes. Do not let flames flare and burn the meat. Once ribs are fully cooked, baste the ribs with barbeque sauce, letting sauce soak into the meat. Watch ribs, as the sauce will burn. Remove from grill. *Hint: You may wrap ribs in foil and place in a warm (not hot) oven until ready to eat.*

BARBEQUE SAUCE FOR THE BACKYARD

Ingredients:

1/2 Cup White Vinegar	2 Tablespoons Onion, Finely Chopped
2 Cups Ketchup	1 Tablespoon Worcestershire Sauce
1/2 Cup Honey	2 Tablespoons Lemon Juice
1/2 Cup Water	1/2 Teaspoon Tabasco® Sauce

Directions:
Put all ingredients into a saucepan and bring to a boil stirring occasionally. Reduce heat and simmer.

No firecracker could rival the excitement "cleaning off a rib bone" could evoke, and no dip in a pool could cool off a 95° day like a generous scoop of homemade peach ice cream.

BBQ Baked BEANS

Ingredients:
1 (3 Pound) Can Baked Beans
1/2 Cup Brown Sugar
2 Tablespoons Yellow Mustard
1/4 Cup Onion, Finely Chopped
1/2 Cup Barbeque Sauce
3 Strips Bacon (Optional)

Directions:
Preheat oven to 350 degrees. In a casserole dish mix beans, brown sugar, mustard, onion, and barbeque sauce. Mix well. Place bacon across the top. Bake for 30 minutes or until bubbly. Makes about 15 servings.

POTATO SALAD
See "Down Home/Church Picnic" Section, page 41 for the Recipe.

Cole Slaw

Ingredients:
1 Small Head Cabbage
1/2 Chopped Green Pepper
1/2 Chopped Red Pepper
1 Bunch Green Onions
2 Grated Carrots
Cole Slaw Dressing

Directions:
Cut cabbage in quarters, grate, and place in a bowl. Chop the green onions and add to cabbage along with the chopped green and red peppers. Add the grated carrots. Mix well and toss with Cole Slaw dressing. Serves 8 to 10.

COLE SLAW DRESSING

Ingredients:
1/4 Cup Ketchup
1/4 Cup Sweet Pickle Relish
1 Cup Mayonnaise

Directions:
Combine all ingredients. Mix well and refrigerate.

DEVILED EGGS
See recipe in the "Down Home/Church Picnic" section, page 40.

Peach
COBBLER

COBBLER CRUST
Ingredients:

4 Cups Flour
2 Teaspoons Salt
2 Cups Vegetable Shortening

1/2 Cup Cold Water
1 Egg Beaten
Peach Pie Filling (recipe follows)

Directions:

Combine flour and salt, then mix in wet ingredients. Blend well with hands. Using hands, form balls (one for bottom crust, one for lattice top).

Roll out ball of crust on floured surface. Roll dough over on rolling pin. Place pin over 9x13 inch glass baking dish and roll into pan. Cut out any excess that overlaps pan. Use excess dough to patch any holes in the crust in the dish.

PEACH FILLING
Ingredients:

2 Cups Water
1 1/2 Cups Sugar
1/4 Cup Flour
2 Teaspoons Cinnamon
1/2 Teaspoon Nutmeg

2 (1 Pound) Bags of Frozen Sliced Peaches
(6 Cups Fresh Blueberries Can Be Substituted for Peaches)
1 Stick Butter

Directions:

Combine water, sugar, flour, cinnamon, and nutmeg. Bring to a boil, and lower heat. Add peaches and butter. Cook and stir until thickened. Pour into crust. Roll out second part of dough into lattice strips and arrange over peach filling. Bake at 400 degrees until top strips are brown and filling is bubbly.

Limeade

Ingredients:
1/2 Cup Fresh Lime Juice
1 Cup Sugar
2 Quarts Water

Directions:
Mix ingredients in a large pitcher.

Hint: Add 2 cups of club soda for effervescence.

Peach ICE CREAM

Ingredients:

2 1/4 Cups Sugar	2 Pints Whipping Cream
6 Teaspoons Flour	4 1/2 Teaspoons Vanilla Flavoring
1/2 Teaspoon Salt	4 Cups Crushed Peaches (Frozen
5 Cups Milk	Peaches, Thawed and Crushed)
5 Eggs, Beaten	1/2 Cup Sugar

Directions:

Mix sugar, flour, salt, and milk in large sauce pan. Stir over low heat for 15 minutes. Slowly add beaten eggs to hot mixture (temper eggs first by slowly adding a little of the hot milk mixture to them). Cool, then add cream and vanilla.

Add crushed peaches which have been sweetened with the half cup of sugar. Stir and freeze in hand cranked or electric ice cream freezer following manufacturer's directions. Serves 8 to 10.

Church TEAS

FRAPPÉ PUNCH

PIMENTO CHEESE SANDWICHES

TEA CAKES

HAM MOLD WITH CRACKERS

TUNA MOLD WITH CRACKERS

SUGAR COOKIES

ORANGE MUFFINS

CHEESE RING

When the Mayweathers joined Metropolitan Baptist Church in Memphis, they gave of their talents, as well. (In fact, shortly after Beneva's death, the church formally dedicated its kitchen area in her honor.) On many occasions, Beneva prepared the food for special events at Metropolitan, and all four daughters participated in church-sponsored activities.

One of the well known activities at the church, and at many churches in Memphis, was the International Tea. Each church represented a country, and funds raised through these events supported Owen College and LeMoyne College (later to merge). It was a highly anticipated event, and congregations worked hard each year to best other church bodies for the coveted first prize. The fun in doing the event was surpassed only by the cause it served - helping young students to go to college.

Frappé
PUNCH

Ingredients:
1/2 Gallon Sherbet (Desired Flavor)
2 Liters Lemon Lime Carbonated Beverage
2 Liters Ginger Ale
Ice Cubes

Directions:
Place sherbet in punch bowl. Pour lemon-lime soda and ginger ale over sherbet. Put ice cubes in mixture to chill. Serves 15 to 20.

Pimento Cheese
SANDWICHES

Ingredients:
2 Pounds Sharp Cheddar Cheese, Grated
1 (7 ounce) Jar Chopped Pimento
1 Small Onion (Chopped)
1/2 Cup Sweet Pickle Relish
1/2 Cup Top Quality Mayonnaise

Directions:
Blend all ingredients in a food processor. Refrigerate. Make sandwiches or serve on crackers. Refrigerate leftover pimento cheese.

Tea
CAKES

Ingredients:
2 Cups Sugar
1 Cup Softened Butter
6 Egg Yolks
1 Tablespoon Vanilla
1 Teaspoon Baking Soda
1/3 Cup Buttermilk
4 Cups All-Purpose Flour

Directions:

Cream sugar with butter. Add egg yolks one at a time and beat until light and fluffy. Add vanilla. Stir baking soda into buttermilk, and alternate with flour to mixture, beating after each addition.

Drop dough by spoonful onto very lightly greased baking sheet and bake at 350 degrees for 8 to 10 minutes or until edges are lightly browned. Makes 3 to 4 dozen.

Ham Mold
WITH CRACKERS

Ingredients:

4 Cups Ham, Chopped Finely
2 Tablespoons Sweet Pickle Relish
1/4 to 1/2 Cup of a Top Quality Mayonnaise *(enough to moisten)*
2 Tablespoons Chopped Pimento
Parsley
Crackers

Directions:

Mix chopped ham, relish, mayonnaise, and pimento in a bowl. Form into desired shape on a serving dish. Chill for at least 1 hour. Garnish with parsley and serve with crackers.

Tuna Mold
WITH CRACKERS

Ingredients:

2 Cans Albacore Tuna
1/4 Cup Chopped Celery
1 Teaspoon Finely Chopped Onion

2 Boiled Eggs
1/4 Cup of a Top Quality Mayonnaise
Dash of Tabasco® Sauce
Crackers

Directions:

Place all ingredients in a bowl, and mix well. Brush mold pan with cooking oil. Fill mold with tuna mixture and chill overnight. Turn onto serving dish. Place crackers around mold on serving dish.

Sugar COOKIES

Ingredients:
2 Sticks of Butter, Softened
1 Cup Sugar
1 Egg
1 1/2 Cups Plain, Unsifted Flour
1 Teaspoon Vanilla

Directions:
Cream butter and sugar. Add egg and mix until well creamed. Add flour and vanilla.

On a greased cookie sheet, drop 1 teaspoon of batter 2 inches apart.

Bake in oven at 375 degrees about 7 to 9 minutes until they are light brown. Remove from oven. Remove cookies immediately from cookie sheet. Makes about 4 dozen.

❖ *These cookies are thin and delicate. Remove from the oven when they begin to turn brown around the edges.*

Orange MUFFINS

Ingredients:

2 Cups All-Purpose Flour
3 Teaspoons Baking Powder
3/4 Teaspoon Salt
2 Tablespoons Sugar
1 Egg
1 Cup Milk
4 Tablespoons Butter (1/4 Cup), Softened
Grated Peel of 1 Orange

Directions:

Preheat oven to 400 degrees. Grease large, 6-muffin pan.

Sift dry ingredients. Combine egg, milk and butter and pour into dry mixture. Stir gently only to moisten. Do not beat. Add grated orange peel.   Fill muffin cups 2/3 full. Bake 20 to 25 minutes or until golden brown. Remove muffins immediately from pan.

Cheese
RING

Ingredients:

1 Pound Sharp Cheddar Cheese, Grated
1 Cup Pecans, (Finely Chopped)
1 Small Onion, Grated
1/2 Teaspoon Tabasco® Sauce
1/2 Cup Top Quality Mayonnaise
1 Small Jar Strawberry Preserves (Or Your Favorite Preserves)

Directions:

Combine all ingredients except preserves and mix well. Press into a ring shaped mold. Refrigerate and let chill at least 2 hours. Before serving, put the preserves in the center of the mold. Serve with fine crackers or wafers.

The Bones. The Mayweathers.
Brothers-in-Law. Sisters-in-Law.
Cousins. Nieces. Nephews.

Imagine the coming together of family from Arkansas, Memphis, Chicago, Detroit, Gary, Atlanta - and as the train conductor used to say, "Parts North!" In times like this, Beneva relied on foods that worked in large quantities. Spaghetti, baked beans and barbeque can go far, and filling up a hungry bunch of "kinfolks" is no small feat!

 Connoisseurs note : OK, OK. We understand that spaghetti is the pasta, not the sauce. But in the South, spaghetti means the whole kit and caboodle, the sauce, the meat, the works. And we do put in the works! We won't even go into baking it with cheese smothered on top...

Family REUNIONS

SPAGHETTI

BBQ CHICKEN

BBQ SHOULDER

BBQ BAKED BEANS

MACARONI SALAD

SEVEN LAYER SALAD

LEMON ICE

PINEAPPLE UPSIDE DOWN CAKE

Spaghetti

Ingredients:
1 (16 Ounce) Package Spaghetti Noodles
Cooking Spray or 1 Tablespoon Olive Oil
1 Onion, Chopped
1 Green Bell Pepper, Chopped
4 Stalks Celery, Chopped
2 Pounds Hamburger
3 (15 Ounce) Cans Tomato Sauce (Or 6 Cups Sauce)
1 (15 Ounce) Can Diced Tomatoes
1 Tablespoon Italian Seasoning
1/4 Teaspoon Sugar
Salt and Pepper to Taste

Directions:
Boil spaghetti noodles according to package directions.
Drain and set aside.

Lightly spray or add oil to pan or deep skillet. Sauté onion, bell
pepper, and celery. Add ground beef to skillet. Brown, season, and
crumble. Drain. Add tomato sauce, diced tomatoes, and Italian
seasoning. Stir in sugar. Simmer for 30 minutes. Either mix sauce
with noodles or spoon sauce over noodles. Makes 8 to 10 servings.

BBQ
CHICKEN

Ingredients:
Split Chicken (Halves)
Favorite Marinade
BBQ Sauce (see BBQ Shoulder
recipe following this one)

Directions:
Wash chicken. Using your favorite marinade, let chicken marinate in refrigerator overnight. To grill, place chicken on oil-coated grill over hot coals, turning frequently. Test thickest pieces for doneness.
Right before removing chicken, brush with BBQ sauce (see recipe below). When sauce is hot, remove from the grill as the sauce will burn.

Barbeque Sauce
See recipe on next page.

BBQ
SHOULDER

Ingredients:

1 1/2 to 2 Pound Pork Shoulder
1/2 to 1 Cup Vinegar
1 Teaspoon Seasoning Salt

1/2 Teaspoon Pepper
2 Tablespoons Worcestershire Sauce
Barbeque Sauce

Directions:

Marinate shoulder overnight in vinegar, salt, pepper, and Worcestershire sauce. Discard marinade. Place shoulder on barbeque grill and cook for about 2 hours over medium hot coals until done, checking frequently. Toward the end of grilling, baste meat frequently with sauce, being careful not to let meat burn.

BARBEQUE SAUCE

Ingredients:

2 Cups Ketchup
1/2 Teaspoon Crushed Red Pepper
1 Tablespoon Worcestershire Sauce
1 Tablespoon Tabasco® Sauce
1 Teaspoon Liquid Smoke

1 Teaspoon Yellow Mustard
1/2 Cup White Vinegar
1/2 Cup Honey
1/2 Cup Water
3 Tablespoons Dark Brown Sugar

Directions:

Mix all ingredients over low heat. Yields approximately 4 cups.

❖ For all meats, remember to discard all marinade after using.

Macaroni SALAD

Ingredients:

1 (16 Ounce) Package Elbow Macaroni
4 Hard-Boiled Eggs, Grated
1 Small Jar Chopped Pimento, Drained
2 Tablespoons Sweet Pickle Relish
1 Tablespoon Chopped Green Pepper
1 Cup of a Top Quality Mayonnaise
1 Teaspoon Sugar
Salt and Pepper to Taste

Directions:

Cook macaroni noodles and drain. Mix macaroni noodles with the remaining ingredients. Chill for several hours before serving. Makes 6 to 8 servings.

BBQ BAKED BEANS
See "4th of July" Section, page 92 for the Recipe.

Seven Layer
SALAD

Ingredients:

Iceberg Lettuce, Shredded
3 Stalks Celery, Chopped
1 Green Bell Pepper
2 Bunches Green Onions Diced
1 (10 ounce) package frozen English Peas,
   Cooked and Drained
6-8 Slices Bacon, Cooked and Crumbled

6 Eggs, Boiled and Sliced
Salt
Pepper
1 Cup of a Top Quality Mayonnaise
1 Tablespoon Sugar
Cheddar Cheese, Grated

Directions:

In a large, glass dish layer ingredients in order listed. Sprinkle with salt and pepper. In a small bowl, mix mayonnaise and sugar and pour over salad. Cover with grated cheddar cheese.

Refrigerate overnight or long enough for the dressing to be absorbed. Serve chilled. Serves 6 to 8.

Lemon ICE

Ingredients:

1 Quart Water
1 1/2 Cups Sugar
1 Cup Strained Lemon Juice *(4 to 6 Lemons)*

1/4 Teaspoon Salt
1 Egg White

Directions:

In a saucepan, boil water and sugar for 2 minutes. Set aside. When cool, add lemon juice and salt. Fold in egg white. Freeze in an electric freezer or a hand cranked freezer following manufacturer's instructions.

Pineapple
UPSIDE DOWN CAKE

Ingredients:

TOPPING:
1/2 Cup Butter
1 Cup Firmly Packed Brown Sugar
1 Cup Chopped Pecans
1 (15 1/2 ounce) Can of Pineapple Slices, Undrained
6 to 8 Maraschino Cherries

CAKE:
1 1/2 Sticks Butter, Softened
1 Cup Sugar
2 Eggs
1 1/2 Cups Sifted Cake Flour

1 Teaspoon Baking Powder
1/2 Cup Milk
2 Teaspoons Vanilla Extract

Directions:

Melt butter in a 9-inch cast-iron skillet. (Make sure cast-iron skillet is well seasoned or cake may stick. A non-stick 10-inch cake pan may be used.) Sprinkle brown sugar and pecans over melted butter. Arrange pineapple slices and cherries over brown sugar mixture; set skillet aside.

Cream butter and sugar; add eggs, mixing well. Sift flour and baking powder together and add to butter/egg mixture alternating several times with milk. Add vanilla. Mix well and carefully pour over pineapple mixture in the skillet. Bake at 350 degrees for 20 to 25 minutes or until toothpick inserted into cake comes out clean. Remove from oven and let cake remain in the skillet for 5 minutes. Hold a plate tightly over the skillet and invert the cake onto the plate. Pineapple mixture will be on top. Remove any pineapple or cherries that remained in the skillet and arrange on the cake.

Hint: There will be extra cake batter remaining. This may be used to make cupcakes or a small Upside Down Pineapple Cake!

Elegant

ENTERTAINING

THE DAYS AT
THE CLUB

Attending to the needs of her husband and family gave Beneva great satisfaction. Yet, like others who are born to nurture, she touched many other people with her kind and compassionate approach.

Many of those who remember her were both members and staff at the Memphis Hunt and Polo Club, a well known and established country club in the eastern part of the city.

She began her career there preparing salads under the watchful eye of the beloved Mr. Ned, the very capable and experienced club chef. Mr. Ned, as everyone called him, was happy to share his expertise with her since she had demonstrated both a talent for food preparation as well as an eagerness to learn. In essence, the Club became Beneva's "culinary academy" of sorts, and it provided her the chance to hone her talents while working on the job.

For some, it would have beeen drudgery, but for Beneva, it was a passion fueled by her love of the art of cooking.

In time, she became Mr. Ned's assistant, and after his death, she was promoted to the position of chef. These were the years during the 1960s and '70s, and work meant seven days a week with a rare day off here and there. For some, that would have been drudgery, but for Beneva, it was a passion fueled by her love of the art of cooking. It also provided work for family and friends. Nieces, nephews and close relatives worked there, and significantly, it provided all four daughters their first real job.

At the Memphis Hunt and Polo Club, there was an understood philosophy of excellence, with no compromising. All knew, "Only the best will do!" For Beneva, this allowed her to work, literally, in a cook's paradise, with the best of everything - including ingredients. Butter, cream and the best cuts of meat were used. Mayonnaise and dressings were made by her or by the staff. Specialty items were often flown in from New York and other cities, and every detail was handled with efficiency and taste. (No wonder she initially found it difficult when starting her own business, since a limited operating budget was unfamiliar to her! But more on that later. . .)

It was a way of doing things, and it laid the groundwork for her approach to cooking - excellence in ingredients and excellence in service. The elegant Thursday night dinners, the casual poolside lunches and the after-church Easter brunches all held her trademark.

Yet even with this responsibility as a chef, she remained ever the nurturer, continuing to attend to the needs of others while pampering those she loved. She often helped fellow staff members with family reunions, church functions and other occasions calling for food. While the Club was closed on Thanksgiving and Christmas, on the eve of these days, many of the members would order dishes to carry home so that they would be able to enjoy Beneva's touch at their holiday tables.

Never able to say "no," on days when children were not allowed at the pool, she often fed members' children who lived nearby and who pedaled by the back door of the Club. Many a kid consumed one of Beneva's hefty hamburgers or hot dogs while steering a bike with one hand! (Lucky for her, it remained unknown to the Club's manager! Let's say it was a good investment in what are today's community leaders!)

Family members who worked with her offer many more stories about her skills, but the most evident quality that surfaces is her generosity. Staff and Hunt and Polo Club members alike remember her pleasure in making sure everyone was fed. No request was too difficult; no menu too tricky. To her children, her friends and all who knew her, these were genuine qualities that never changed.

It would be these qualities that would lift her into the next phase of her life , while establishing her name citywide as the wonderful Chef of the Memphis Hunt and Polo Club.

Thursday
NIGHT DINNER

FILET MIGNON WITH
HORSERADISH SAUCE

SQUASH CASSEROLE

FRESH STEAMED
ASPARAGUS

SPINACH SALAD

CREAMED MUSHROOMS

CRESCENT ROLLS

CHOCOLATE SOUFFLÉ WITH
WHIPPED CREAM &
CHOCOLATE SAUCE

A dinner reservation for the evening out meant Thursday night at the Club. Unlike other meals, such as quick lunches or a light brunch when dishes were prepared upon order, the Thursday night fare was a little more involved.

Filet
MIGNON
with Horseradish Sauce

Ingredients:
1 Filet per Person
Salt
Pepper
Soy Sauce
Cooking Spray

Directions:
Lightly spray frying pan with a cooking spray. In the heated pan (hot but not smoking), sear the meat on both sides to seal in juices. Season the filet with salt, pepper, and soy sauce. Transfer to the oven and cook at 450 degrees to desired doneness; 10 to 15 minutes for rare.

Hint: A meat thermometer for this and other meat dishes may be used to indicate if the cut is rare, medium or well done.

HORSERADISH SAUCE
Ingredients:
1 Cup of Sour Cream
1 Tablespoon of Horseradish Sauce
1/2 Teaspoon of Worcestershire Sauce

Directions:
Mix ingredients and blend well. Serve with the filet mignon.

"Unlike other meals, the Thursday night fare was a little more involved..."

Squash CASSEROLE

Ingredients:

6 Yellow Crookneck Squash   1/4 Cup of Sugar
1 Small Onion, Chopped   1 Teaspoon of Salt
1 Stick of Butter   1 Cup of Herbed Stuffing Mix

Directions:

Wash and slice squash. Place the squash in a pot, and cover with water.
Add onion to pot. Boil until tender (about 15 to 20 minutes). Drain well.

Place squash mix in a bowl, then chop with metal spatula. Add butter, sugar,
salt, and herbed stuffing mix. Place in a casserole and bake at 350 degrees
for 25-30 minutes.   Makes 4 to 6 servings.

Fresh Steamed ASPARAGUS

Ingredients:

1 Bunch Fresh Asparagus
Butter

Directions:

Cut fresh asparagus spears about 4 inches from the bottom. Place flat in
pan of water and cover with foil. As soon as water comes to a boil, boil
for 1 minute. Drain water. Put butter over asparagus and serve. (For those
with steamers, follow the manufacturer's instructions.)
Enough for 4 or 5 servings.

Spinach Salad
WITH DRESSING

Ingredients:
1 1/2 Pounds Fresh Spinach
3 Hard Boiled Eggs, Chopped
1 (8 Ounce) Can Sliced Water Chestnuts
6 Slices of Fried, Crisp, and Crumbled Bacon
1/2 Red Onion, Sliced in Thin Rings

Directions:
Wash spinach in cold water, carefully examining leaves. Tear large leaves into smaller pieces. Combine spinach pieces with other ingredients, and toss lightly with dressing. Makes 4 to 6 servings.

DRESSING
Ingredients:
1/2 Cup Vegetable Oil
1/3 Cup Sugar
1/4 Cup Vinegar
2 Tablespoons Sherry
1 Teaspoon Salt
1 Teaspoon Paprika
1 Teaspoon Dark Steak Sauce
1 Tablespoon of Minced Green Onions

Directions:
Combine all ingredients, and mix thoroughly.

Creamed
MUSHROOMS

Ingredients:
1 Pound Mushrooms
1 Stick Butter
1 Tablespoon Flour
1/2 Cup Whipping Cream
1 Tablespoon Sherry
Salt
White Pepper

Directions:
Wipe mushrooms clean. Discard stems. Sauté mushroom caps in butter. While still in the pan, sprinkle the flour over the mushrooms. Pour in whipping cream and add sherry. Add salt and pepper to taste. Lower heat and stir gently as sauce thickens. Makes 4 servings.

Crescent ROLLS

Ingredients:

2 Cups Milk (Scalded)
1/4 Cup Butter
1/4 Cup Sugar
1 1/2 Teaspoons Salt

2 Tablespoons Yeast
1/4 Cup Water
5 to 6 Cups All-Purpose Flour, Sifted
Melted Butter

Directions:

Combine scalded milk, butter, sugar, and salt. Cool to lukewarm.

Soften yeast in lukewarm water; stir and combine with cooled milk mixture; add half the flour; beat well. Add enough of the remaining flour to make a soft dough; mix thoroughly.

Turn out on lightly floured board and knead about 10 minutes, until smooth and satiny. Place dough in a warm, greased bowl; brush surface very lightly with melted butter; cover with a towel and let rise in a warm place (80 to 85 degrees) about 2 hours or until doubled in bulk.

Roll dough into a large circle about 1/4 inches thick. Cut into wedge-shaped pieces, and roll each in jelly-roll fashion, beginning at the round edge. Place on a greased baking sheet with the point of the dough on the bottom.

Curve each roll into crescent shape on a greased baking sheet; cover and let rise until doubled in bulk. Brush with melted butter.

Bake 15 to 20 minutes in a moderate oven at 375 degrees.
Makes 2 dozen rolls.

Hint: Make sure water is neither too warm nor too cool, as the wrong temperature will have an adverse effect on the yeast.

Chocolate
SOUFFLE
WITH WHIPPED CREAM AND CHOCOLATE SAUCE

Ingredients:

1/3 Cup Flour
1/2 Cup Sugar
1/8 Teaspoon Salt
1 Cup of Milk

4 Eggs, Separated
1/4 Teaspoon Cream of Tartar
1 Teaspoon Vanilla
2 Squares (2 Ounces) Unsweetened Chocolate,
Melted

Directions:

Combine flour, sugar, salt in a saucepan. Stir in milk a little at a time.

Cook over low heat, stirring constantly, until mixture is smooth and thick. Stir melted chocolate into thickened milk mixture.

Beat yolks until thick and yellow; fold in the milk mixture.
Let the mixture cool.

Beat egg whites until foamy; sprinkle the cream of tartar over them and continue beating until stiff but not dry. Fold into the first mixture with vanilla.

Pour into an ungreased casserole (1 1/2 quarts). Bake at 325 degrees 50 to 60 minutes or at 425 degrees for about 25 minutes or until well browned, using a lower shelf in the oven. The long, slow baking makes a soufflé of even moistness throughout; quick baking gives a thicker crust and a soft moist interior.

Serve immediately from the baking dish. Top servings with whipped cream and chocolate sauce. Serves 4 to 6.

CONTINUED

WHIPPED CREAM

Ingredients:
2 Cups of Heavy Whipping Cream
1/4 Cup Confectioners' Sugar
1 Tablespoon Brandy

Directions:
Using a mixer, whip the cream on the highest setting until the cream is firm. Gently stir in the confectioners' sugar and brandy.

CHOCOLATE SAUCE

Ingredients:
1/4 Cup of Butter
2 Squares (2 ounces) Unsweetened Chocolate
1 (5 ounce) Can Evaporated Milk
1 Cup of Sugar
1 Teaspoon of Vanilla
1 Teaspoon of Instant Coffee

Directions:
Melt butter and chocolate in a sauce pan. Stir in milk, sugar, vanilla, and coffee. Stir until well-blended.

Cook 10 to 15 minutes over medium heat, stirring constantly until thick and smooth.

Sunday DINNER

WELSH RAREBIT (APPETIZER)

BABY RACK OF LAMB
WITH MINT SAUCE

FRIED EGGPLANT

HERBED GREEN BEANS

BROILED TOMATOES

GREEN SALAD WITH
POPPY SEED DRESSING

POTATO ROLLS

CHARLOTTE RUSSE

As part of her training,

Beneva planned a menu to

incorporate the elements that

attract us to good food.

Colors, textures and the blending

of flavors add up to greater appeal

and enjoyment. The following

menu, although relatively simple,

was both pleasing to the eye and

satisfying to the taste buds.

Welsh Rarebit
APPETIZER

Ingredients:
3 Tablespoons Butter
3 Tablespoons Flour, Sifted
1/2 Teaspoon Salt
Dash of Pepper
1/2 Cup Milk
1/4 Cup Sherry
1 1/2 Cups Shredded Sharp Cheddar Cheese
1 Cup Beer
Toast Points

Directions:
Melt butter in large double boiler. Blend in flour and season with salt and pepper. Pour milk in gradually, stirring until mixture thickens, about 10 minutes. Remove from heat. Slowly add sherry. Stir about five minutes or until thick and smooth. Add shredded cheese, stirring until melted and smooth. Stir in beer slowly.

If desired, reheat over low heat for a few minutes.
Serve immediately over toast points.

(For toast points: Remove crusts from buttered bread slices, toast and cut into triangles.)

Baby
RACK OF LAMB

Ingredients:

Have Butcher Trim and Prepare 2 Racks of Lamb

Directions:

Rub marinade over lamb, cover and refrigerate 2 to 3 hours. Remove from refrigerator.

Place racks of lamb on hot grill and grill 5 to 7 minutes on each side for medium rare. The lamb will be brown on all sides. Remove from the grill, and place in 350 degree oven for 5 minutes to cook further only if desired. Remove from oven and cut into desired servings. Serve with purchased mint sauce. Serves 6 to 8.

MARINADE

Ingredients:

2 Cups of a Top Quality Mayonnaise
2 Tablespoons of Rosemary
1/2 Cup of Butter, Softened
2 Tablespoons of a Dijon Mustard

Directions:

Mix ingredients blending thoroughly.

Fried EGGPLANT

Ingredients:
1 Medium Eggplant
1 Cup Flour
2 Eggs, Well Beaten
1 Cup Milk
1 Cup of Your Favorite Prepared Fish Coating Mix
(the kind used for frying)
Oil
Salt

Directions:
Mix eggs and milk.

Peel eggplant; cut in half crosswise, and then cut lengthwise into
1/2 inch thick slices. *(The slices should be the size of thick French fries.)*
Roll each slice in flour: dip in the egg mixture and then roll in the
coating mix.

Heat cooking oil. Deep-fry eggplant in hot cooking oil until golden
brown. Sprinkle with salt. Serve immediately. Makes 4 to 6 servings.

Herbed GREEN BEANS

Ingredients:
2 Pounds of Fresh Green Beans
1 Teaspoon of Salt
1/4 Cup Olive Oil
4 Tablespoons of Butter, Melted
1 Teaspoon Sugar
Garlic and Herb Seasoning to Taste

Directions:
Wash beans, snap off ends and remove strings. Bring a half pot of water to a boil (or enough water to cover beans). Add salt. Drop in beans and let cook on high 5 to 10 minutes until crisp tender. Drain; season beans with olive oil, butter, sugar and herb seasoning. Toss the beans to allow seasoning to mix in thoroughly. Makes 4 to 6 servings.

Broiled TOMATOES

Ingredients:
4 to 6 Medium Tomatoes
Butter (Melted)
Parmesan Cheese
Seasoned Bread Crumbs

Directions:
Peheat oven to 450 degrees. Slice tomatoes in half. Top tomatoes with melted butter, Parmesan cheese, and bread crumbs. Place in a small Pyrex dish or pie pan. Bake at 450 degrees about 5 minutes.

Green Salad with
POPPY SEED DRESSING

Ingredients:

1 Pound Spinach
2 to 3 Heads of Bibb Lettuce
1 (11 Ounce) Can Mandarin Orange Sections, Drained
1 (14 Ounce) Can Hearts of Palm, Sliced
1 Small Purple or Red Onion, Thinly Sliced (Optional)
Poppy Seed Dressing

Directions:

Wash, pick, and break up greens. Wrap greens in paper towel and chill in refrigerator. When ready to serve, place greens in salad bowl. Add oranges, hearts of palm, and onion. Add about half of the poppy seed dressing and toss. Reserve the other half for guests who wish more dressing on their salads. Serves 6 to 8.

POPPY SEED DRESSING

Ingredients:

2 Tablespoons Poppy Seeds   3/4 Cup of Vegetable Oil
1 Tablespoon Minced Onion   1/3 Cup Honey
1 Tablespoon of a Dijon Mustard   1/4 Cup Red Wine Vinegar
1/2 Teaspoon Salt

Directions:

Combine all the ingredients in an electric blender.
Process on low speed for 30 seconds. Cover and chill.

Stir well before serving.

Charlotte
RUSSE

Ingredients:

2 Envelopes of Unflavored Gelatin
3/4 Cup Sugar
1/4 Teaspoon Salt
4 Eggs, Separated
2 Cups Milk, Scalded
2 Cups Heavy Cream, Whipped
1/3 Cup Brandy
12 Lady Fingers, Split
9 Strawberries
Heavy Cream, Whipped, for Garnish

Directions:

Combine gelatin, sugar, and salt in a double boiler. Add egg yolks and slowly stir in milk. Cook, stirring constantly, until mixture coats spoon. Let mixture cool, fold in whipped cream. Add 3 tablespoons of brandy and refrigerate until mixture congeals slightly.

Sprinkle remaining brandy over lady fingers and line the spring pan or soufflé dish with the lady fingers. Gently pour the cooled mixture into the pan.

Refrigerate at least 8 hours. Remove from mold and garnish with strawberries and whipped cream. Serves 6 to 8 for dessert.

Potato ROLLS

Ingredients:

1 Cup Milk, Scalded
1/2 Cup of Lukewarm Water
5 Cups All-Purpose Flour
2 Eggs, Beaten
Melted Butter

2 Tablespoons Yeast
2/3 Cup Butter
1/2 Cup Sugar
1 1/2 Teaspoons Salt
1 Cup Mashed Potatoes

Directions:

Combine scalded milk, butter, sugar, salt, and mashed potatoes; cool to lukewarm.

Soften yeast with lukewarm water; stir and combine with cooled milk mixture; add about half the flour; add the beaten eggs and beat well. Add enough of the remaining flour to make a soft dough; mix thoroughly.

Turn out on a lightly floured board and knead about 10 minutes, or until smooth and satiny.

Place dough in a warm greased bowl. Brush surface very lightly with melted butter. Cover with a towel and let rise in a warm place (80 to 85 degrees) for about 2 hours or until dough has doubled in bulk. Turn out on a board and shape into rolls.

Place cut rolls on greased baking sheet. Let rise until they double in size. Brush with melted butter. Bake at 375 degrees 10 to 15 minutes.

Hint: Make sure water is neither too warm nor too cool, as the wrong temperature will have an adverse effect on the yeast.

Poolside
LUNCH

CHEF SALAD WITH
1000 ISLAND DRESSING

HOT DOGS WRAPPED
IN BACON

CHEESEBURGERS

FRENCH FRIES

COFFEE ICE CREAM

Whether you are lounging poolside at a private club, or sitting at the water's edge watching your children play in a familiar country creek, the sound of people enjoying the water on a hot day is a classic summertime tune. There is something about a cool dip in the water that's a sparkle for both mind and body, and when a quick swim is added, that's even better! Add a classic summertime lunch and you have the ingredients for a perfect sunny afternoon.

Chef Salad with
1000 ISLAND DRESSING

Ingredients:
1 Bunch Romaine Lettuce (Torn into Bite Size Pieces)
2 Tomatoes Cut into Wedges
1/2 Cup Chopped Celery
2 Cups Cooked Ham Strips
2 Cups Cooked Chicken Strips
2 Cups Cheddar Cheese, Sliced Into Thin Strips
4 Hard Boiled Eggs (Sliced)
8 to 10 Slices Crispy Fried Bacon

Directions:
Combine all ingredients except bacon strips and toss lightly. Top each
salad serving with two slices of crisp bacon. Serve with Thousand Island
Dressing. Serves 4.

THOUSAND ISLAND DRESSING

Ingredients:
2 Cups of a Top Quality Mayonnaise
1/4 Cup Celery, Chopped
2 Tablespoons Ketchup
1/4 Cup Sweet Relish

Directions:
Mix ingredients and serve. Remaining dressing should be refrigerated.

Hot Dogs
WRAPPED *with* BACON

Ingredients:
Thick Beef Hot Dogs (1 per person)
Bacon Slices, Uncooked
Sharp Cheddar Cheese, Cut Into 3-Inch Strips
Buns

Directions:
Slit hot dog to form a pocket and insert 2 cheese strips. Wrap each hot dog with a slice of bacon and hold with a tooth pick. Deep fry and serve on a bun.

*Cheese*BURGERS

Ingredients:

Ground Chuck	Worcestershire Sauce
Chopped Onion	Cheddar Cheese
Salt	Hamburger Buns
Pepper	

Directions:
For each burger, use 1/4 pound of ground chuck and one teaspoon of chopped onion. (May substitute ground round or ground beef) Season to taste using salt, pepper, and Worcestershire sauce. Grill to desired doneness, and add a slice of sharp cheddar before removing from the grill.

Serve on buns.

French FRIES

Ingredients:

4 Potatoes
Salt
White Pepper
Oil

Directions:

Cut four potatoes lengthwise (peeled or unpeeled) into strips.
Fry a small amount at a time in deep hot oil for six to
seven minutes or until crisp and golden.

Drain on paper towels; sprinkle with salt and white pepper.
Serve hot. Serves 4.

Coffee ICE CREAM

Ingredients:

6 Cups Half and Half
8 Cups Heavy Whipping Cream
2 Cups Sugar
1 Cup Instant Coffee
1 Tablespoon Vanilla

Directions

Mix all ingredients. Stir until blended. Freeze, using an electric or hand-
cranked ice cream freezer. To serve, spoon out into individual dishes.
Makes 10 to 12 servings.

Bridge
CLUB

TOMATO SURPRISE

CHICKEN SALAD

MARINATED VEGETABLES

ASSORTED CRACKERS
AND WAFERS

PEPPERMINT ICE CREAM
WITH CHOCOLATE SAUCE

In the card room at the Club each Tuesday and Wednesday, the ladies matched wits and skill as cards moved across the table, while plates of Mother's famous chicken salad and tomato surprise moved from table to table.

As years passed, she would cater a number of bridge parties in homes and other locations. Bridge offered an afternoon or evening of good fun and conversation for all who came.

Tomato
SURPRISE

Ingredients:

4 Tomatoes (1 per Person)
1 Cup Chopped Celery
4 Teaspoons Chopped Fresh Parsley

Homemade Mayonnaise
Seasoned Salt
1/2 Cup Green Onions

Directions:

Cut off the tops of the tomatoes and carefully scoop out pulp. Mix all of the above ingredients with the tomato pulp and add seasoned salt to taste. Equally divide the mixture and stuff into scooped out tomatoes. Top with homemade mayonnaise.

HOMEMADE MAYONNAISE

Ingredients:

2 Egg Yolks
1 1/2 Cups Vegetable Oil
2 Tablespoons of Lemon Juice
3/4 Teaspoon of Dry Mustard

1/2 Teaspoon Salt
Dash of Paprika
3 Drops Tabasco® Sauce

Directions:

Beat egg yolks in a mixing bowl at high speed until thick and lemon colored. Add oil 1 tablespoon at a time, and beat until mixture begins to thicken. Gradually add lemon juice, beating until thickened. Add remaining ingredients, stirring well. Spoon mayonnaise into a glass container only. Use immediately or seal in an airtight container. Refrigerate and use within 2 days.

Do not store in a metal container!

Chicken
SALAD

Ingredients:
6 Cups Chopped, Cooked Chicken or Turkey Breast
1 Cup Chopped Celery
4 Hard-Boiled Eggs, Grated
1 Cup of a Top Quality Mayonnaise
4 to 6 Drops Tabasco® Sauce
Salt and Pepper to Taste

Directions:
Combine chicken, celery, eggs, mayonnaise, Tabasco®, salt and pepper.
Cover and chill.

CHICKEN FOR CHICKEN SALAD
Ingredients:
4 Boneless Skinless Chicken Breasts
1 Onion
2 Large Stalks of Celery
Salt

Directions:
Boil chicken breasts (or turkey breasts if you choose) with onion, celery,
and salt until done, about 20 to 30 minutes. Drain and chill.

Marinated VEGETABLES

Ingredients:

1 (15 ounce) Can Baby Carrots

1 (15 ounce) Can Whole Green Beans

1 (15 ounce) Can Baby English Peas

Vinaigrette Dressing, Purchased

Directions:

Drain all canned vegetables. Place vegetables in bowl and mix with a purchased vinaigrette dressing of your choice. Refrigerate for 2 hours.

Marinated vegetables may be garnished with a dollop of homemade mayonnaise on top.

Peppermint ICE CREAM

Ingredients:

8 Cups Whipping Cream

6 Cups Half and Half

8 Cups Crushed Peppermint Sticks

1 Tablespoon Vanilla

For Best Results, Use Peppermint Sticks Only

Directions:

Beat or crush peppermint sticks. Mix whipping cream and Half & Half. Add crushed peppermint and allow peppermint to dissolve in the cream mixture. Add vanilla and freeze using an electric or hand cranked ice cream freezer.

CHOCOLATE SAUCE

Ingredients:

2 Tablespoons Hot Water

1/4 Cup Whipping Cream

2 Squares Unsweetened Chocolate

1 Cup Sugar

1 Tablespoon of Vanilla

Directions:

Combine all ingredients except vanilla in a saucepan over medium heat. Stir continuously until mixture thickens (about 10 minutes). After mixture cools, stir in vanilla.

Debutante NIGHT

SHRIMP ON ICE WITH
COCKTAIL SAUCE

SMOKED SALMON WITH
CAPERED CREAM CHEESE

TURKEY HASH ON
TOAST POINTS

SAUSAGE LINKS AND
CANADIAN BACON

CREAMED EGGS

HOT CURRIED FRUIT

MINIATURE CHEESECAKES

CHOCOLATE DIPPED
STRAWBERRIES

One of the more special nights at the Club was the presentation of debutantes. The music seemed to swell each time a beautiful ballroom dress swirled across the floor. Everyone smiled at the faces of proud fathers tightly holding their daughters' hands, while holding even tighter the little girls they did not want to let go.

For the debs, the evening would be a long one, complete with the main ball and the many after parties that had been scheduled. The menu would consist of light, yet attractive foods that complemented the gaiety of the evening.

Shrimp on Ice
with COCKTAIL SAUCE
(HORS D'OEUVRE)

Ingredients:
2 Pounds Unpeeled Fresh Shrimp
2 Stalks Celery, Cut
1 Lemon, Juiced, Reserving Peel
1 Tablespoon Pickling Spice

Directions:
Place shrimp, cut celery (stalks and leaves), the juice from the lemon, the lemon, and the pickling spices in cold water in a large saucepan. Bring to a boil and cook 2 to 3 minutes.

Drain and cool with cold water and ice. Peel, devein, chill, and serve with cocktail sauce.

SHRIMP SAUCE
Ingredients:
2 Cups Ketchup
1 Teaspoon Lemon Juice
2 Tablespoons Horseradish Sauce
1 Teaspoon Worcestershire Sauce
1 Tablespoon Chopped Celery
2 or 3 Drops of Tabasco® Sauce

Directions:
Combine ingredients. Stir, mix well, and chill. Serve with fresh shrimp.

Smoked Salmon with
CAPERED CREAM CHEESE
(HORS D'OEUVRE)

Ingredients:

Purchased Smoked Salmon of
Choice, Already Sliced
1 (8 Ounce) Package Cream Cheese
2 Tablespoons Capers

Juice of 1 Lemon
1 Tablespoon Chopped Onion
Cracked Pepper
Deli Party Pumpernickel Bread

Directions:

Mix cream cheese, capers, the juice of 1 lemon, and chopped onion. Spread cream cheese mixture on deli-party pumpernickel bread. Add a slice of salmon on cream cheese, and top with cracked pepper. Serves 15 to 20.

Turkey HASH

Ingredients:

1 Large Stalk of Celery, Finely Chopped
1 Green Bell Pepper, Finely Chopped
1 Onion, Finely Chopped
1/2 Stick Butter
1/2 Cup Flour
1/2 Cup Cream or Half and Half
3 Cups Chicken Broth (1 1/2 Cans)

3/4 Cup Sherry (Do not use cooking sherry)
6 Cups Turkey, Diced
Salt
White Pepper
Tabasco® Sauce
Toast Points

Directions:

In a large skillet on medium high heat, cook the celery, green pepper and onion in the butter. When softened, add the flour and continue cooking for 3 minutes, stirring constantly. Add the Half and Half, broth and sherry and bring to a boil. Whisk until thickened and add turkey. Add salt, white pepper and Tabasco® to taste. Serve over toast points.

(To make toast points remove crusts from buttered bread slices, toast and cut into triangles.)
Makes 4 to 6 servings.

Creamed EGGS

Ingredients:

4 Tablespoon Butter
4 Tablespoon All-Purpose Flour
2 Cups Half and Half
2 Teaspoons Salt
1/2 Teaspoon White Pepper

2 Cups Sharp Cheddar
12 Boiled Eggs, Grated
2 Cups Buttered Bread Crumbs
Paprika

Directions:

Cream butter and flour until smooth over medium heat. Gradually stir in Half and Half, stirring constantly until thickened. Add salt, pepper and cheese and set aside. When mixture cools, stir in eggs and pour into a baking dish. Top with buttered bread crumbs and a few shakes of paprika. Bake uncovered 25 to 30 minutes in a 350 degree oven until top is brown. Makes 4 to 6 servings.

Hot Curried FRUIT

Ingredients:

1 (16 ounce) Can Peach Halves
1 (16 ounce) Can Pear Halves
1 (8 ounce) Can Apricot Halves
2 (8 ounce) Cans Chunk Pineapples

1 Small Jar Maraschino Cherries
2 Sticks Butter
2 Cups Brown Sugar
1/2 Teaspoon Curry Powder

Directions:

Drain all fruit, and place fruit in large saucepan. Add butter, brown sugar, and curry powder. Heat slightly until desired warmth. Serve warm.

Miniature
CHEESECAKES

Ingredients:

24 ounces Cream Cheese, Softened
1 Cup of Sugar
5 Eggs
1 Teaspoon Vanilla
Blueberries, Peaches, Strawberry or Cherry Preserves
(or fresh version of fruit)

Directions:

Mix cream cheese, sugar, eggs, and vanilla in mixer. Fill miniature foil cups 3/4 full. Bake on cookie sheet for 15 to 20 minutes at 350 degrees. Let cool.

Dot each miniature cheesecake with fruit topping (preserves or fresh) as desired. Makes 4 to 5 dozen.

Chocolate Dipped
STRAWBERRIES

Ingredients:
Fresh Strawberries
Molding (Dipping) Chocolate (used for coating and making candy)*

Directions:
Dip fresh strawberries in chocolate coating (follow directions for melting the coating). Set the dipped strawberries on wax paper. Allow to cool. Strawberries may be refrigerated.

*Hint: This chocolate can be found in specialty stores or where cake baking supplies are sold. It can also be found in some grocery stores, usually during the strawberry harvest season or during the holidays. Follow directions on the package for best results.

CHOCOLATE SAUCE

Ingredients:
2 Squares Chocolate
1 Cup Sugar
1/2 Cup Whipping Cream
1/4 Cup Water
1 Teaspoon Vanilla

Directions:
In a double boiler combine chocolate, sugar, cream, and water. Mix well. Cook over medium heat until chocolate has melted. Stir constantly until thick and smooth. Mix in vanilla. Sauce may be used warm or cool.

Easter
BRUNCH

CHICKEN-A-LA-KING

CHEESE GRITS

APPLE RINGS

SAUSAGE PATTIES

BACON

BISCUITS

CINNAMON ROLLS

A long-held tradition among many parishes and congregations is the Easter sunrise service. Beautiful in its meaning, the service reflects the commitment and the sincerity of those who hold these beliefs.

142

For those who attend these early services, as well as those who enjoy rising later in the morning, a mid-morning feast is a welcome treat! Many Club members looked forward to this annual brunch with its family favorites such as cheese grits and cinnamon rolls. For us, it was also a special time. What other children got the chance to dye 60 to 70 dozen eggs for the annual Easter Egg Hunt? As Beneva's children, we would dye the eggs and the members would hide them on the grounds. Later, we'd laugh at our red, green and purple fingers at the end of the day. Beneva would chuckle, too.

That was a happy time for us. Believe it or not, we still get red, green and purple fingers on Easter. . .

Chicken-a-la KING

Ingredients:
1/2 Cup Butter
1/2 Cup Green Pepper, Cut in Thin Strips
1 Cup Sliced Mushrooms
4 Tablespoons Flour
1 Cup Chicken Stock
1 Cup Milk
1/2 Cup Cream
1/4 to 1/2 Cup Sliced Pimento
3 Cups Diced Cooked Chicken
Salt
Pepper
2 Slightly Beaten Egg Yolks
2 to 3 Tablespoons Sherry (Optional)

Directions:
Heat butter. Add green pepper and mushrooms. Cook over low heat about 5 minutes or until soft. Add flour and stir until blended; slowly add stock and milk. Stir over low heat until thick and smooth. Add cream, pimiento, and chicken; season to taste. Heat thoroughly.

Stir a little of the hot sauce into the slightly beaten egg yolks; slowly add to remaining sauce stirring constantly. Add sherry. Serve immediately on buttered toast points. (Cut decrusted bread into triangles and toast.)

Serves 3 to 4.

Cheese
GRITS

Ingredients:
4 Cups Water
1 Cup Grits
1/2 Teaspoon Salt
2 Cups Sharp Cheddar Cheese, Grated
1 Stick Butter (1/2 Cup)

Directions:
Slowly stir grits and salt into boiling water. Reduce heat.
Cook 5 to 7 minutes or until thickened. Add 2 cups of
grated sharp cheddar cheese and 1 stick of butter Stir well.
Serve hot. Serves 6 to 8.

Apple RINGS

Ingredients:
4 Cooking Apples
1/4 Teaspoon Cream of Tartar
2 Cups Sugar
1 1/2 Cups Water
2 Teaspoons Cinnamon
1/2 Cup Raisins
1/2 Cup Chopped Nuts

Directions:
Wash and dry 4 cooking apples. Cut a small slice from the stem end.
Do not peel. Remove the core and slice the apple into rings.
Arrange in a baking dish.

Mix sugar, cream of tartar and water. Place over low heat until sugar is dissolved
stirring constantly (6 to 8 minutes). Bring to a boil and stir in cinnamon and raisins.
Boil 3 minutes stirring occasionally. Pour over apple rings and garnish with nuts. Bake
10 minutes in a 400 degree oven. Serve hot. Serves 6 to 8.

Biscuits

Ingredients:
2 Cups Sifted All-Purpose Flour
3 Teaspoons Baking Powder
1/2 Teaspoon Salt
3 Tablespoons Shortening
3/4 to 1 Cup Milk

Directions:
Preheat oven to 450 degrees.
Sift dry ingredients into a large bowl. Cut in the shortening with a
pastry blender. Add milk, blending quickly until dry
ingredients are moistened.

Turn onto a lightly floured surface. *(Dough should be soft.)*
Knead gently 10 to 12 strokes. Roll or pat dough 1/2 inch thick.
Dip 2 1/2 inch biscuit cutter in flour; cut into dough straight down.

Bake on a lightly greased baking sheet at 450 degrees for about 12 minutes.

Cinnamon
ROLLS

Ingredients:

2 Cups Water
1 Stick Butter (Quarter Pound)
1/2 Cup Shortening
3/4 Cup Sugar
1 1/2 Teaspoons Salt
2 Tablespoons Yeast (2 Packages)

2 Eggs, Slightly Beaten
6 Cups Flour, Sifted
1 Stick Butter, Melted
1/4 Cup Cinnamon
2 Cups Sugar

Directions:

Boil Water. In a mixing bowl, combine 1 1/2 cups of the boiling water, 1 stick of butter, shortening, 3/4 cup sugar, and salt. Using a bread hook or flat beater, mix until lukewarm. Soften yeast in remaining 1/2 cup lukewarm water. Add eggs to first mixture (butter, shortening, etc.), and then add yeast, mix well. Add sifted flour and blend well to make a soft dough. Sprinkle with flour, cover, and refrigerate, allowing dough to rise (2 hours). Combine cinnamon and 2 cups sugar. Set aside.

Divide dough into 3 or 4 workable portions. Beginning with first portion, roll out dough, brush with melted butter, and sprinkle with the sugar and cinnamon mixture. Roll into log shape, slice evenly (about an inch), and place on greased cookie sheet. Repeat with remaining portions. Let rolls rise 10 to 15 minutes. Bake at 400 degrees for 10 to 15 minutes until lightly browned. Glaze while warm. Yields 4 to 5 dozen rolls.

GLAZE

Ingredients:

1 Pound Box Powdered Sugar
3 Tablespoons Milk

Directions:

Mix powdered sugar and milk into a paste (adjust more or less milk for consistency). The glaze will melt down over the hot rolls.

Brownies

Ingredients:
4 Squares Unsweetened Chocolate
1 1/2 Stick Butter
2 Cups Sugar
4 Eggs
1 1/3 Cup Plain Unsifted Flour
1 Teaspoon Baking Powder
1 Teaspoon Vanilla

Directions:
Melt chocolate and butter in sauce pan. Let cool. In a mixer, beat eggs and sugar well. Combine chocolate and egg mixture. Add flour, baking powder, and vanilla. Pour into a greased cookie sheet. Bake at 350° for 15 to 20 minutes. Icing brownies while hot.
Yields - 3 dozen.

KAHLUA ICING
Ingredients:
4 Squares Unsweetened Chocolate
1 Stick Butter
4 Cups Powdered Sugar
Half and Half
1 Tablespoon Kahlua

Directions:
Melt chocolate and butter. Let cool. In a mixing bowl, combine chocolate mixture and sugar. Add half and half until desired spreading consistency is reached. Add Kahlua and spread over brownies.

· C A T E R I N G ·
Southern
HOSPITALITY

Our mother spent much of the 1960s, '70s and '80s at the Memphis Hunt and Polo Club. While she'd often prepared special dishes for members to carry home for their events and parties, she'd never entertained the thought of actually catering a party on her own. So understandably, when approached by a member to cater an event, she was apprehensive.

With encouragement from the member, however, and with renewed confidence and reassurance that she could indeed carry it out, she took the assignment and the party was a success!

As more requests came, she soon began a small catering activity on the side while continuing to fulfill her duties at the Club. Yet she never lost her loyalty, and even though the demand for her services grew, her duties as the Club's chef still remained a priority with her.

continued

CATERING

*Southern*HOSPITALITY

There were times when she would start dinner at the Club, go to one of the outside parties, then return to the Club in time to prepare dessert. In fact, some the members used to label her "the magician" since she seemed to be in two places at once! As children, we often called her "the magician" because she cooked so fast that if you blinked, the food was done!

As others referred their friends and colleagues to her catering services, and as the physical and mental pressure of maintaining both responsibilities mounted, the demand grew to a point where she had little choice but to move on. With our father's help, she made the decision to branch out on her own, and Mayweather Catering Service, Incorporated was born. Even though her clientele was already established, more and more Memphians, as well as clients from throughout the entire Mid-South, were added to the list.

Throughout the years, after watching and working with our mother, we have come to realize that catering, although demanding, is indeed unique. What other profession allows you to be a part of special moments shared by family and friends? In what other line of work can you witness rites of passage, and learn about cultures and traditions? What other profession allows you to see some of the most beautiful homes, buildings and gardens ever?

And then there is the heartwarming benefit of providing services to generations of family members for christenings, Bar and Bat Mitzvahs, teen parties, weddings, anniversaries and more. A loss in a family that our company has served for years is a loss to us, as well.

« MAYWEATHER » CATERING INC »

A successful party was work, but as we look back on it— it was the time of our lives...

And let's not forget our "real family" - our staff. All of the work provided by our mother's catering company could have not been possible without the help of a very supportive and loyal staff. For us, the women and men who worked with our mother became our aunts, uncles, cousins, sisters and brothers - in fact, most of our friends actually thought staff were our relatives! This group had known Beneva for years, first working together at the Club, then working alongside her in her business. Some of our most joyous times came in our mother's work kitchen when only the whirr of the mixers or the rumble of the ice machines could drown out the jokes and laughter from these warm, wonderful people.

But when it was business...it was business. The business of making lists, getting out the food, packing dishes and utensils, and meeting party times was hectic. A successful party was work, but as we look back on it, it was the time of our lives. . .

Mayweather Catering, Incorporated took a great deal of hard work, dedication, and organization, but it represented the best of our Mother's talents. The dishes were legendary and the service unequalled, but she continued to explore new ideas and new ways of preparation. The following are a few of the many menus that she used.

$\mathcal{M}$ayweather Catering, Incorporated took a great

deal of hard work, dedication and organization,

but it represented the best of our Mother's

talents. The dishes were legendary and the

service unequalled, but she continued to explore

new ideas and new ways of preparation, as well as

following the traditions that served her well. The next

few pages are a sampling of the many menus that she used.

Brunches
& LUNCHES

SEAFOOD QUICHE

BENEVA'S CRUSTY BACON

HOT SAUSAGE
& EGG CASSEROLE

TOMATO ASPIC

MARINATED ASPARAGUS

CHEESE BISCUITS

STRAWBERRY BREAD

LEMON SOUFFLÉ WITH
RASPBERRY SAUCE

Brunch has always been a favorite for club meetings, get-togethers and pre-wedding parties. Traditional breakfast foods combined with fruit, breads and beverages are always popular.

Brunch could almost be defined as "breakfast taken a step further" since it does indeed give you the feeling of breakfast with the long lasting effect of lunch!

In this section, there are a number of dishes that can be used for a brunch or a luncheon. Beneva's Crusty Bacon has long been a favorite of ours.

Seafood
QUICHE

Ingredients:
1 (9-inch) Pie Crust*
3/4 Cup Swiss Cheese, Shredded
1/2 Pound Shrimp, Chopped
1/2 Pound Crabmeat
1 Small Onion, Chopped
2 Eggs
1 Cup Half and Half
1/2 Teaspoon Salt
Dash Ground White Pepper
Dash Nutmeg
*(*Purchased, or see recipe under "Down Home/Church Picnic" on page 42)*

Directions:
Place pie crust in pan.
Sprinkle cheese, seafood, and onion onto crust.
Mix eggs, Half and Half, salt, white pepper and nutmeg.
Pour egg mixture over cheese, seafood, and onion.
Bake uncovered at 325° F for 45 minutes or until
a toothpick inserted in the center comes out clean.
Let stand for a few minutes.
Slice and serve. Serves 4 to 6.

Beneva's
CRUSTY BACON

Ingredients:
3 Eggs
1/2 Cup Milk
1/4 Teaspoon Dry Mustard
1 Pound Thick Rind Bacon
Cracker Crumbs

Directions:
Beat eggs with milk and dry mustard. Dip each slice of bacon in the egg mixture. Roll bacon in cracker crumbs. Place bacon on cookie sheet and bake at 400 degrees until crispy – 15 to 20 minutes. Bacon needs to be turned once during baking.

Hot Sausage
& EGG CASSEROLE

❖ *For the recipe, see the "At Home on Provine Street / After Prom Party" section on page 69.*

Tomato ASPIC

Ingredients:

2 Tablespoons (2 Envelopes) Unflavored Gelatin
1/2 Cup Cold Water
2 1/2 Cups Canned Tomato-Vegetable Juice
1 Tablespoon Minced Onion
1 Tablespoon Sugar
1 Teaspoon Salt
4 Whole Black Peppers
1 Bay Leaf
4 Cloves
2 Tablespoons Lemon Juice
1 Stalk Celery, Chopped
1 Tablespoon Worcestershire Sauce

Directions:

Soften gelatin in water. Heat tomato-vegetable juice and add
gelatin, stirring until dissolved. Add remaining ingredients.
Strain mixture, pressing well to extract the flavors of the
ingredients. Pour liquid into mold, and let cool. Refrigerate
until congealed.
To serve, turn mold onto bed of lettuce. Put mayonnaise in
center. Makes 4 to 6 generous servings.

Marinated
ASPARAGUS

Ingredients:
1 Bunch Fresh Asparagus
1 Cup Italian Dressing
Pimento or Red Bell Pepper Strips (Optional)

Directions:
Cut about 3 inches off the bottom of the asparagus. Wash asparagus, place in a pot and cover with water. Bring to a boil, and steam asparagus for about 3 minutes, leaving the asparagus with a crunchy texture. Drain. Place ice on asparagus to cool. After cooling, place in a shallow dish and cover the asparagus with the Italian dressing or your favorite vinaigrette dressing. Place a top on the dish or cover with plastic wrap. Refrigerate. Before serving, chill the serving plate. Garnish the asparagus with pimento or red pepper if desired.
Makes 4 servings.

Cheese BISCUITS

Ingredients

2 Cups Sifted All-Purpose Flour
3 Teaspoons Baking Powder
1/2 Teaspoon Salt
3 Tablespoons Shortening
1 Cup Sharp Cheddar Cheese, Grated
3/4 to 1 Cup Milk

Directions

Preheat oven to 450 degrees. Sift dry ingredients into a large bowl. Cut in shortening with a fork. Add grated cheddar cheese and add milk, blending quickly until dry ingredients are moistened. Turn onto lightly floured surface (dough should be soft). Knead gently 10 to 12 strokes. Roll or pat dough 1/2 inch thick. Dip 2 1/2-inch biscuit cutter in flour; cut dough straight down. Bake on lightly greased baking sheet at 450 degrees about 12 minutes.
Makes 10-12 biscuits.

Strawberry
BREAD

Ingredients:

1 Cup Butter, Softened
1 1/2 Cups of Sugar
1 Teaspoon Vanilla Extract
1 Teaspoon Lemon Extract
4 Eggs, Beaten
3 Cups Flour
1 Teaspoon Salt
1 Teaspoon Cream of Tartar
1/2 Teaspoon Baking Soda
1 Cup Strawberry Preserves
1/2 Cup Sour Cream
1 Cup Pecans

Directions:

Cream butter and sugar together. Add vanilla and lemon extract. Stir in eggs. In another bowl, sift dry ingredients. Combine preserves and sour cream, and add to egg mixture, and combine with dry ingredients. Mix in pecans. Fill 2 greased and floured loaf pans. Bake at 350 degrees for 45 to 50 minutes.

Lemon
SOUFFLE

Ingredients:

1 Envelope Unflavored Gelatin
1/4 Cup Cold Water
5 Eggs, Separated
3/4 Cup Fresh Lemon Juice

Grated Rind of 1 Lemon
1 1/2 Cup Sugar
1 Cup Whipping Cream

Directions:

Sprinkle gelatin over cold water to soften. Mix together egg yolks, lemon juice, rind, and 3/4 cup sugar. Place in double boiler, stirring constantly until thickened. Remove from heat. Stir in gelatin until dissolved. Cool mixture over ice. Beat egg whites until they begin to hold shape. Gradually add the remaining 3/4 cup sugar until egg whites are stiff. Whip cream until stiff peaks form. Fold egg whites and cream into yolk mixture until no white streaks remain.
Pour into a 2 quart soufflé dish and chill overnight.

Before serving, remove from mold and serve with raspberry sauce.

RASPBERRY SAUCE
Ingredients:
1 Box Frozen Raspberries
1/2 Cup Confectioner's Sugar

Directions:

Thaw raspberries. Place in food processor or blender. Strain to remove seeds. Stir confectioner's sugar into strained raspberries. Refrigerate and serve. Makes 4 to 6 servings.

Bar/Bat
MITZVAH

SALMON WITH GREEN SAUCE

LATKES

SWEET NOODLE KUGEL

ROAST BEEF AND
BLEU CHEESE SALAD

SPICY SPINACH

ORANGE GLAZED CARROTS

BAGELS

TRIFLE

CHOCOLATE POUND CAKE

LEMON TARTS

Beneva loved doing these celebrations of life. She often remarked that they were not just catering assignments, they were lessons in culture and tradition. She learned so much from these rites of passage and throughout her career, she looked forward to each and every one.

They also allowed her to show her creativity while cooking in the large quantities that she was so accustomed to preparing. It was not unusual to have two or three hundred people at these occasions. The staff of her catering company also enjoyed these celebrations which were joyous occasions for children, family and friends.

Salmon with GREEN SAUCE

Ingredients:
Side of Salmon
1 Stick Melted Butter
1 Cup Sherry
Juice of 2 Lemons
Salt

Directions:
Place salmon, skin side down, on foil which has been coated with butter. Pour remaining melted butter, sherry, and lemon juice over salmon. Sprinkle lightly with salt. Cover with foil. Bake at 350 degrees for 15 to 20 minutes.

Cool and remove from foil. Garnish and serve with green sauce.

GREEN SAUCE
Ingredients:
2 Cups of a Top Quality Mayonnaise
1/4 Cup Frozen, Chopped Spinach, Cooked, Drained, and Cooled
1 Teaspoon Fresh Lemon Juice
1 Tablespoon Chopped Onion

Directions:
Blend all ingredients in food processor. Serve with Salmon.

Latkes

Ingredients:
4 Potatoes
1 Egg
1/2 Cup Finely Chopped Onion
2 Tablespoons Flour
Salt
Pepper
Butter

Directions:
Peel potatoes and grate. Combine grated potatoes, 1 slightly beaten egg, onion, flour (and more if needed to bind) and salt and pepper to taste. Mix well.

Shape into 6 patties. Melt butter in saucepan or skillet. Brown slowly in butter, about 5 minutes on each side. Drain on paper towels.

Sweet Noodle
KUGEL

Kugel Ingredients:
8 Ounce Package Egg Noodles, Cooked and Drained
1 Cup Butter, Melted
6 Eggs, Beaten
1 Cup Sugar
2 Cups Half and Half
2 Cups Apricot Nectar
2 Teaspoons Vanilla

Topping Ingredients:
1 1/3 Cups Corn Flake Crumbs
1/2 Cup Butter, Melted
2 Teaspoons Cinnamon
1/2 Cup Sugar

Directions:
Mix all Kugel ingredients and pour into greased 9x13 glass baking dishes. Mix all topping ingredients and sprinkle on top of kugel.

Kugel will be very loose (lots of liquid) so be careful when putting in oven. Bake at 350 degrees for at least an hour.
Serve warm or at room temperature. Makes 8 to 10 servings.

Roast Beef &
BLEU CHEESE SALAD

Ingredients:

2 Tablespoons Sesame Oil
2 Tablespoons Vegetable Oil
3 Cups Thinly Sliced, Cooked
   Roast Beef, Trimmed
2 Medium Carrots, Julienned

1 Cup Sliced Mushrooms
1 Red Bell Pepper, Thinly Sliced
Bleu Cheese Dressing
Mixed Salad Greens

Directions:

Heat the sesame oil and vegetable oil in large skillet over medium-high heat. Add the beef, carrots, mushrooms, and bell pepper. Cook until heated through, tossing to coat evenly with the oil.

Combine the beef mixture with the Bleu Cheese dressing in a bowl and mix lightly. Spoon onto mixed greens on serving plates. Makes 3 to 4 servings.

BLEU CHEESE DRESSING

Ingredients:

1/2 Cup Bleu Cheese
1/2 Cup of a Top
   Quality Mayonnaise
1/4 Cup Sour Cream
1 Tablespoon Vinegar

1 Tablespoon Worcestershire Sauce
Dash of Tabasco® Sauce
Freshly Ground Pepper

Directions:

Mix well all ingredients except Tabasco® Sauce and ground pepper. Season with Tabasco® Sauce and freshly ground pepper to taste. Chill until serving time. Serve on salad.

Spicy SPINACH

Ingredients:

2 Boxes Frozen Chopped Spinach
1 Stick Butter
1/2 Cup Seasoned Bread Crumbs

1/4 Cup Grated Onions
2 Cups Jalapeno Pepper Cheese
Salt

Directions:

Boil spinach and drain well. Add butter, bread crumbs, onion, and cheese. Season with salt to taste. Mix well. Place in one quart glass baking dish. Bake for 20 to 25 minutes or until heated thoroughly.

Orange GLAZED CARROTS

Ingredients:

1 Package Baby Carrots
1 Cup Sugar
1 Cup Water
1 Stick Butter
1 Orange, Sliced

Directions:

Boil carrots, drain, and place in casserole dish. Make syrup by combining sugar and water. In saucepan boil sugar and water for 5 minutes. Add butter and orange slices. Boil an additional 2 minutes.

Pour syrup over carrots. Place in oven and bake at 350 degrees for 20 to 30 minutes. Remove orange slices before serving. Serve warm. Serves 4.

Trifle

Ingredients:

Bourbon Whisky, To Taste
Boiled Custard
2 Teaspoons Vanilla
1 Jar Raspberry Preserves
Sponge cake, Sliced in Strips

Fresh Raspberries
Whipped Cream
Slivered Almonds
Maraschino Cherries

Directions:

Add bourbon to cold boiled custard. Stir in 2 teaspoons of vanilla. Spread preserves over cake strips. Layer half of the cake in bottom of trifle bowl, and cover with half of the custard. Sprinkle fresh raspberries over the custard. Repeat layers. Cover and refrigerate at least 24 hours to allow cake to season.

Before serving, top with whipped cream, a sprinkle of almonds, and cherries. This will serve 8 to 10 people.

BOILED CUSTARD

Ingredients:

1 Cup Sugar
1 Tablespoon All-Purpose Flour
3 Eggs, Well Beaten
4 Cups Milk, Scalded

Directions:

In saucepan, mix sugar with flour and add eggs, beating well. Gradually add hot milk, stirring until blended. Pour into double boiler and cook until mixture coats spoon, stirring constantly.

Chocolate POUND CAKE

Ingredients:
1/2 Pound Butter, Softened
1/2 Cup Vegetable Shortening
3 Cups Sugar
5 Eggs
3 Cups Sifted Cake Flour
1 Teaspoon Baking Powder
1/3 Cup Cocoa
1 Cup Milk

Directions:

Cream butter, shortening, and sugar until fluffy; beat in eggs. Sift dry ingredients together; Add to creamed mixture alternately with milk. Mix well. Pour batter into large greased and floured tube pan. Bake at 300 degrees for 1 hour and 30 minutes. Serve with whipped cream and chocolate sauce.

(See Beneva's Chocolate Sauce in "Elegant Entertaining / Bridge Club Parties" Page 135.)

Lemon
TARTS

CRUST

Ingredients:

3/4 Cup Butter, Softened
2 (8 Ounce Packages) Cream Cheese
2 Cups Sifted Flour
Dash Salt

Directions:

Combine ingredients in mixing bowl. Pinch off piece of mixture and roll into ball. Continue to make as many balls as mixture allows. When completed, press balls into metal tart cups or a miniature muffin pan. Bake at 325 degrees for 25 minutes. Cool and remove.

FILLING

Ingredients:

1/2 Cup Fresh Lemon Juice
Grated Rind of 2 Lemons
2 Cups Sugar
1 Cup Butter
4 Eggs, Beaten

Directions:

In a double boiler, combine lemon juice, rind, and sugar. Add butter. Heat over boiling water until melted. Add eggs. Continue to cook for approximately 15 minutes or until thick. Let filling chill.

Fill tarts just before serving. Tarts may be garnished with whipped cream.

Caterers, florists and bakery owners everywhere consider weddings as the anchor of their business. No other celebration requires as much planning and detail, and no other event depends so much on the food and beverages served!

The activities in Beneva's kitchen during the day before a wedding were priceless. Many of the treasured moments of our childhood came from watching our mother and her staff give endless detail to hors d'oeuvres and fancy dishes. They had a pride in their craft that could not be surpassed.

Wedding RECEPTIONS

SPICY STUFFED SNOW PEAS

PECAN SANDWICHES

MUSHROOMS WITH SAUSAGE OR CHEESE

CAVIAR PIE AND TOAST ROUNDS

CUCUMBER SANDWICHES

BEEF TENDERLOIN WITH ROLLS

Spicy Stuffed
SNOW PEAS

Ingredients:
2 Cups Pecan Halves
2 Teaspoons Cayenne Pepper
24 Snow Peas
1 Cup Cream Cheese

Directions:
Sprinkle pecans with pepper and roast in oven at 350 degrees for 10 minutes. Remove and let cool.

Take snow peas, snap off stems, and remove strings. Blanche snow peas in boiling water for approximately 1 minute. Drain; dip in ice bath (ice and water) to cool and to stop the cooking process.

Finely chop the pecans, mix the pecans with cream cheese. Using sharp paring knife open one side of a blanched snow pea and stuff with pecan mixture. Repeat process for all snow peas. Chill and serve.
Makes 10 to 12 servings.

Pecan SANDWICHES

Ingredients:

2 Pounds Bacon, Uncooked
1 Green Bell Pepper, Cut and Cored
1/2 Cup of a Top Quality Mayonnaise

1 Cup Pecans
1 Loaf Very thin sliced Whole Grain Bread

Directions:

Fry bacon until crispy. Drain on paper towels.

Chop bacon, green bell pepper and pecans separately in a food processor. Mix together with mayonnaise. Spread mixture thinly on bread. Trim edges and slice into fourths. Place on desired serving dish and serve.

Mushrooms STUFFED *with* SAUSAGE

Ingredients:

10-20 Medium Mushrooms
1 Pound Hot Sausage

2 Tablespoons Chopped Green Onions
2 Tablespoons Plain Bread Crumbs

Directions:

Remove stems from mushrooms and wipe each mushroom with a towel. Mix sausage, onions, and bread crumbs. Roll into small balls and stuff into center of mushroom. Place on cookie sheet, sausage side up, and bake at 400 degrees for 15 to 20 minutes until sausage is done. *(or: mushroom cap side down)*

Caviar Pie
& TOAST ROUNDS

Ingredients:

6 Hard-Boiled Eggs, Chopped
4 Tablespoons of a Top Quality Mayonnaise
1 Cup Onion, Minced
8 Ounce Package of Cream Cheese

1/3 Cup Sour Cream
1/4 Ounce Jar Caviar
1 Lemon, Sliced
Parsley

Directions:

Mix chopped boiled eggs with mayonnaise. Spread over bottom of greased, 8-inch spring form pan. Sprinkle with onion. Blend cream cheese and sour cream until smooth. Spread this mixture over onions. Cover and chill overnight. Before serving, spread caviar over top. Remove from pan and garnish with lemons and parsley. Serve with crackers. Serves 10 to 12.

Open Face
CUCUMBER SANDWICHES

Ingredients:

3 Cucumbers
Italian Dressing

1 Loaf of White Bread
Top Quality Mayonnaise

Directions:

Peel cucumbers, slice thin. Marinate cucumbers in Italian dressing approximately 15 to 20 minutes.

Cut bread into rounds using a 2 inch round cutter (do not toast bread). Spread light layer of mayonnaise on bread rounds. Place cucumber on top. Garnish with parsley and serve. Serves 20 to 22.

Hint: Assemble just before serving

Beef Tenderloin
WITH ROLLS

Ingredients:
1 Beef Tenderloin, Trimmed
Salt
Pepper
1 Cup Soy Sauce

Directions:
On grill over medium high heat, brown meat approximately 4 minutes on both sides. Remove meat and place on a pan. Salt and pepper both sides. Pour a cup of soy sauce over meat. Bake at 450 degrees until desired doneness; 15 to 20 minutes for medium rare. Slice thin and serve with rolls. Serves 15 to 20.

ROLLS
See "Elegant Entertaining / Thursday Night Dinner" section of the book, page 117.

Formal
DINNER

CRAB CAKES APPETIZER

COLD CUCUMBER AND
DILL SOUP

BIBB LETTUCE SALAD WITH
WALNUTS, MANDARIN
ORANGES & RASPBERRY
DRESSING

BEEF TENDERLOIN WITH
BÉARNAISE SAUCE

CORN PUDDING

TWICE BAKED POTATOES

STEAMED SNOW PEAS

ROLLS

TIRAMISU

We truly believe had she lived, our mother never would have retired. She loved her work...and loved to work. Yet she always expressed to us that what she really loved doing was the formal, seated dinner party that showcased an elegant menu and a beautiful table setting. She felt designing a menu and preparing the settings for a beautiful formal dinner was a dying art that needed reviving.

This menu is an example of one such occasion.

Crab Cakes
APPETIZER

Ingredients:
2 Pounds Fresh Lump Crabmeat, Drained and Flaked
1/2 Cup Plain Bread Crumbs
2 Eggs, Beaten
2 Tablespoons Green Onions, Finely Chopped
1 Teaspoon Dry Mustard
1 Teaspoon Worcestershire Sauce
1/8 Teaspoon Salt
3/4 Cup All-Purpose Flour
Vegetable Oii

Directions:
Combine crabmeat, bread crumbs, eggs, green onions, dry mustard, Worcestershire sauce, and salt, stirring well. Shape into 12 patties (2 inches in diameter); chill well (mixture will be slightly loose).

Flour crab cakes on both sides; fry in hot oil until golden brown, turning once. Drain on paper towels. Serve with a sauce of your choice.

Cold Cucumber
& DILL SOUP

Ingredients:
4 medium or 8 Small Cucumbers, Peeled
2 Teaspoons Salt
1/4 Cup Butter
9 Shallots, Minced
8 Cups Chicken Stock
2 Tablespoons Fresh Dill, Snipped
Fresh Ground Pepper
1 Cup Heavy Cream
Dill and Cucumber Slices for Garnish

Directions:
Cut cucumbers in half, lengthwise, and scoop out seeds with a spoon. Discard seeds. Chop cucumbers coarsely and sprinkle with 2 teaspoons of salt. Set aside in a colander to drain.

Melt butter in saucepan on medium heat. Add shallots to melted butter. Reduce heat and cook, stirring occasionally, until shallots are soft (about 5 minutes). Add chicken stock and dill.

Rinse cucumbers to remove salt before adding cucumbers to the soup. Cook about 5 minutes over medium heat. Cool slightly and puree in blender. Season to taste and chill. Just before eating, stir in cream. Garnish with dill and cucumber slices.
Serves 8 to 10.

Bibb
SALAD

Ingredients:
2 Heads Bibb Lettuce
2 (8 Ounce) Cans Mandarin Oranges
1 Cup Chopped English Walnuts

Directions:
Wash and drain lettuce. Place lettuce on individual salad plates.
Sprinkle with desired amounts of mandarin oranges and walnuts.
Sprinkle with raspberry dressing.

RASPBERRY DRESSING
Ingredients:
2 1/2 Cups Frozen Raspberries, Partially Thawed
4 Tablespoons Lemon Juice
1 Teaspoon Dry Mustard
1/2 Teaspoon Salt

Directions:
In a small bowl or blender, combine all the ingredients.
Blend well. Cover and chill.

Makes about 2 1/2 cups

Beef Tenderloin
WITH BÉARNAISE SAUCE

Ingredients:
1 Beef Tenderloin
1 Cup Soy Sauce
Salt
Pepper

Directions:
On grill over medium high heat, brown meat on both sides. Remove meat and place on a pan. Salt and pepper both sides. Pour a cup of soy sauce over meat. Bake at 450 degrees until desired doneness. Serve with horseradish sauce *(see recipe in "Elegant Entertaining/Thursday Night Dinner", page 113)* or Béarnaise Sauce *(see below).* Slice thick for dinner portions.

BÉARNAISE SAUCE
Ingredients:
3 Egg Yolks
1 Tablespoon Lemon Juice
2 Tablespoons Hot Water
1/4 Teaspoon Salt
Dash Cayenne Pepper or Tabasco® Sauce
1/2 Teaspoon Dried Tarragon
1/2 Cup Butter, Melted

Directions:
In a small heavy sauce pan, mix all ingredients except melted butter. Add melted butter and cook over low to medium heat, stirring constantly until sauce begins to thicken. Remove from heat. Do not overcook.

Corn PUDDING

Ingredients:
4 Cups Fresh Cut Corn or
2 Cups Canned Whole Kernel Corn and
2 Cups Canned Creamed Corn
6 Tablespoons Butter, Softened
1/2 Cup Sugar
4 Eggs, Beaten
3 Cups Whipping Cream
1 Teaspoon Salt

Directions:
Cream butter and sugar in bowl. Add beaten eggs, cream, salt, and mix well. Stir in corn. Pour into a 3 quart buttered casserole dish. Bake at 450 degrees for 15 minutes. Reduce heat to 325 degrees and bake approximately 30 minutes longer until firm. Serves 4 to 6.

Twice Baked
POTATO

Ingredients:
6 Baking Potatoes, Washed and Oiled
1 Pound Bacon, Uncooked
1 Small Jar Pimento, Chopped
2 Tablespoons Parsley, Chopped
1 Stick Butter, Softened
Salt
White Pepper
2 Cups Shredded Sharp Cheddar Cheese

Directions:
Scrub potatoes and spray potatoes with cooking oil spray. Place potatoes on a cookie sheet. Cover the pan with foil and place in a 400 degree oven for about 45 minutes to 1 hour or until soft.

Fry bacon until crispy. Chop bacon in food processor.

Cut potatoes in half lengthwise and scrape out potatoes. Put shells aside to stuff later. Place scooped out potatoes in mixing bowl. Add chopped bacon, pimento, parsley and butter to potato mixture. Beat on medium speed. Add salt and white pepper to taste.

Stuff mixture into potato halves. Place on cookie sheet. Sprinkle with cheese. Before serving, heat potatoes until cheese melts. Serve hot. Makes 12 servings.

Hint: Be careful to leave enough potato for the peel to retain its shape.

Steamed
SNOW PEAS

Ingredients:
2 Pounds Snow Peas
1 Stick Butter
Salt
White Pepper

Directions:
Snap off stems of snow peas and remove strings.
Wash, place in a pot, and cover slightly with water.
Bring peas to a boil; remove immediately from heat and
drain. Add butter, salt, and pepper to taste. Serves 10 to 12.

Yeast
ROLLS

Ingredients:

2 Cups Boiling Water
1 Stick Butter
1/2 Cup Vegetable Shortening
3/4 Cup Sugar
1 1/2 Teaspoons Salt
2 Tablespoons Yeast (2 Packages)
2 Eggs Slightly Beaten
6 Cups Flour, Sifted

Directions:

Boil water. In a bowl, mix butter, shortening, sugar, and salt with 1 1/2 cups of boiling water. Mix until lukewarm. Place remaining 1/2 cup of water in a separate bowl, and when lukewarm, add yeast.

Add beaten eggs to lukewarm sugar and shortening mixture. Add yeast mixture and mix well. Add sifted flour and blend well. Sprinkle with flour, cover, and refrigerate in bowl. Allow dough to rise *(4 hours)*. Roll out dough and cut with pastry cutter. Fold cut out pastry in half and place on a greased cookie sheet. Place on top of stove or oven, and let rolls rise in pan. *(The rolls will almost double in size.)* Remove dough from top of stove or oven, and bake at 400 degrees until brown. Butter the rolls and serve.

Tiramisu

Ingredients:
6 Egg Yolks
1 Cup Espresso or Strong Coffee, Brewed
1/2 Cup Sugar
5 Tablespoons Brandy or Cognac
1 Pound Mascarpone Cheese
6 Egg Whites
3 Dozen Lady Fingers
2 Tablespoons Cocoa

Directions:
Combine egg yolks, 1 tablespoon of coffee, sugar, and
brandy into a large bowl. Beat 2 to 3 minutes.
Add cheese and beat 3 to 5 minutes until smooth.

In another bowl, combine egg whites and a pinch
of sugar. Beat until stiff. Fold into cheese mixture.

Pour rest of coffee into flat dish. Dip one side of each lady finger
in the coffee and layer, wet side up, on the bottom of a 9 by 13-
inch glass dish. Spread 1/3 of cheese mixture over the lady fingers
and sprinkle with cocoa. Continue to layer lady fingers, dipped on
one side with the coffee, spreaded with cheese mixture and
sprinkled cocoa. Refrigerate before serving.

Cocktail
PARTY

WATER CHESTNUTS
WITH BACON

ASPARAGUS ROLLUPS

PORK TENDERLOIN WITH
JEZEBEL SAUCE

SESAME CHICKEN AND
HONEY DIP

ARTICHOKE DIP WITH
PITA BREAD

STUFFED NEW POTATOES

ORANGE SUGAR COOKIES

COCONUT PECAN SQUARES

The cocktail party represents Southern Hospitality at its best. What is better than good conversation, a cool drink and bites of delicious food?

For the caterer, it is important that the guests enjoy a variety of tasty yet easily-held foods, but it is very important that the host and hostess remain relaxed and stress-free. In the end, everyone has a good time, and the hosts and hostesses look good!

Water Chestnuts
& BACON

Ingredients:
1 Can Whole Water Chestnuts
1/4 Cup Brown Sugar
1/4 Cup Soy Sauce
Uncooked Bacon Slices (1 Pound Package)
Toothpicks

Directions:
Drain water chestnuts. Soak water chestnuts in brown sugar and soy sauce mixture for 30 minutes. Cut bacon into halves. Wrap bacon around chestnuts and hold together with toothpick.

Deep fry water chestnuts until crispy. Serve hot.
Serves 6 to 8.

Asparagus
ROLL-UPS

Ingredients:
1 Can Asparagus, Drained
1 Loaf White Bread
2 Cups of a Top Quality Mayonnaise
2 Tablespoons Seasoned Salt
1/4 Cup Melted Butter
Paprika

Directions:
Cut edges from bread slices and flatten slices with rolling pin. Mix mayonnaise and seasoned salt and spread mixture on the flattened slices. Roll 2 or 3 asparagus spears in a bread slice; cut roll-up in half. Repeat with remaining asparagus and bread slices. (Asparagus spears may extend beyond the bread.)

Brush with melted butter; sprinkle paprika over roll-ups. Arrange in baking pan; bake in an oven at 400 degrees until brown.
Serves 10 to 12.

Pork Tenderloin
WITH JEZEBEL SAUCE

Ingredients:
2 Pork Tenderloins
Salt and Pepper
Marinade *(See Below)*

Directions:
Liberally sprinkle tenderloin with salt and pepper on both sides. Pour half of marinade over tenderloin and refrigerate overnight.

Remove meat from marinade; discard marinade. In a hot skillet, brown tenderloin on both sides. Remove tenderloin from skillet and place in pan. Pour remaining marinade over browned tenderloin. Bake in oven for 20 to 30 minutes at 350 degrees. Slice and serve warm with Jezebel Sauce *(see below)*.

MARINADE
Ingredients:

1 Cup Soy Sauce	1 Cup Dry Sherry
2 Tablespoons Honey	1 Teaspoon Thyme
1 Teaspoon Dry Mustard	

Directions:
Mix ingredients well. Pour 1/2 of marinade over tenderloin, reserving remainder to use before baking.

JEZEBEL SAUCE
1 (12 Ounce) Jar Pineapple Preserves
1 (12 Ounce) Jar Apple Jelly
1 Tablespoon Dry Mustard
1/4 Cup Horseradish Sauce

Combine all ingredients. Serve with the tenderloin.

Sesame Chicken
WITH HONEY DIP

Ingredients:

6 Boneless, Skinless Chicken Breasts, Uncooked
2 Cups Buttermilk
Salt
Pepper
Seasoned Salt
2 Tablespoons Toasted Sesame Seeds
Paprika
All Purpose Flour
Cooking Oil

Directions:

Cut chicken breasts into strips (chicken finger size). Wash, drain, and place in a bowl. Pour buttermilk over chicken. Soak overnight.

Remove from refrigerator. Drain buttermilk and discard. Season chicken to taste with salt, pepper, seasoned salt, sesame seeds and paprika. Roll in flour and deep fry in medium hot cooking oil until golden brown. Do not overcook.

HONEY DIP

Ingredients:

2 Cups of a Top Quality Mayonnaise
1/4 Cup Ketchup
1/4 Cup Honey

Directions:

Mix well. Dip is ready to serve.

Artichoke DIP

Ingredients:

2 (8 Ounce) Cans Artichoke Hearts
1/4 Cup Parmesan Cheese
1/4 Cup of a Top Quality Mayonnaise
1 Package Italian Dressing Dry Mix

Directions:

In a food processor, blend artichoke hearts, cheese, mayonnaise, and Italian dressing. Mix well.

Serve hot or cold with toasted pita bread or with crackers

Stuffed NEW POTATOES

Ingredients:

1 Dozen New Potatoes
Vegetable or Cooking Oil
1 Teaspoon Chopped Parsley
1 Teaspoon Chopped Pimento

1/4 Cup Melted Butter
6 Slices Chopped Cooked Bacon *(Fried Crispy)*
Salt and Pepper
1 Cup Grated Sharp Cheddar Cheese

Directions:

Scrub new potatoes clean; rub lightly with oil and bake at 425 degrees for 30 minutes or until soft to the touch. Remove from oven and let cool. Cut potatoes in half, and scoop out potato, leaving enough potato to hold the shape of the potato skin. Place scooped potatoes in mixer and add all of the ingredients except cheese. Place mixture in potato skin shells and top with grated cheddar cheese. Before serving, heat until cheese melts and potatoes are hot.

Orange
SUGAR COOKIES

Ingredients:
2 Sticks Butter, Softened
1 Cup Sugar
2 Eggs
1 1/2 Cups All-Purpose Flour, Unsifted
1/2 Teaspoon Salt
4 Tablespoons Grated Orange Rind
1/2 Teaspoon Orange Extract

Directions:
Cream butter and sugar. Add eggs, and mix until well creamed. Add flour and salt and mix. Add orange rind and orange extract and blend.

On a greased cookie sheet, for each cookie drop 1 teaspoon of the dough. Place about 2 inches apart. Lightly sprinkle each cookie with sugar. Place in oven at 375 degrees and bake for 5 to 7 minutes or until lightly browned. Remove from oven. Remove cookies immediately from the cookie sheet. Makes 2 dozen.

Coconut
PECAN SQUARES

Crust Ingredients:
1/2 Cup Butter, Softened
1 Cup Flour
1/2 Cup Packed Brown Sugar

Directions:
Blend all ingredients well. Pat mixture into a greased
13x9x2 inch pan. Bake crust at 375 degrees for
10 minutes or until lightly browned. Set aside.

Remaining Ingredients
1 Cup Packed Dark Brown Sugar
1/2 Cup Flour
1/2 Teaspoon Salt
1 (3 1/2 Ounce) Can Flaked Coconut
1 Teaspoon Vanilla
2 Eggs
1/2 Cup Chopped Pecans

Directions
Combine above ingredients in bowl using a spoon or your hand, and
then stir mixture well. Spread the mixture over the cooked crust that
you set aside. Bake at 375 degrees for 15 to 20 minutes. Cut into
squares while warm.

Signature
DISHES
(FOR WILD GAME HUNTERS)

SMOKED DUCK QUESADILLAS

DUCK WRAPS

FRIED WILD TURKEY

SAVORY QUAIL

PHEASANT POT PIE

COUNTRY FRIED DUCK

DUCK GUMBO

After catering for some families for two or three generations, we find that they have become what we fondly call "extended families." They present a challenge, for to grow with them we must constantly create new and different menus that change with times as well as tastes. One such challenge for Beneva was to create specialty dishes for a family in which hunting was a favored sport.

She eventually became widely known for this specialty and from that, her signature dishes for wild game were born.

Smoked Duck
QUESADILLAS

Ingredients:
4 Ducks
8 Tortillas (6 inches)
2 Cups Grated Hot Pepper Cheese
Salt
Pepper

Directions:
Wash ducks. Season with salt and pepper. Cook ducks in smoker for an hour to an hour and a half until done. Remove breast meat only. Slice breast meat very thin.

On a greased cookie sheet, lay out 4 tortillas. Divide meat evenly over the 4 tortillas. Sprinkle hot pepper cheese over meat. Top with another tortilla. Bake in a 400 degree oven for 15 minutes or until cheese is melted, and tortilla is slightly brown and crunchy.
Cut quesadillas in quarters and serve.
Serves 12 to 16.

Duck
WRAPS

Ingredients:

3 Duck Breasts
1/2 Cup Italian Dressing
1 Tablespoon Honey

1/2 Pound Sliced Bacon, Uncooked
1 Can Whole Water Chestnuts
Cooking Oil

Directions: Wash ducks

Cut duck breasts into thin strips. Marinate duck strips in Italian dressing and honey for 3 hours.

Cut bacon slices in half. Wrap water chestnuts with duck strips; then wrap bacon slices around duck strips. Stick with toothpick to hold.

Deep fry in medium hot oil until bacon is done. Serve hot.

Fried

WILD TURKEY

Ingredients:

1 Wild Turkey Breast
2 Cups Buttermilk
2 Cups Flour
Salt

Pepper
Seasoned Salt
Peanut Oil

Directions:

Wash wild turkey. Cut the breast of the turkey into small bite size chunks. Marinate meat in buttermilk overnight. Drain buttermilk.

Season turkey with salt, seasoned salt, and pepper. Roll turkey in flour and deep fry approximately 5 to 10 minutes or until done. Serve hot.

Savory QUAIL

Ingredients:
6 to 8 Quail (Allow 2 Per Person)
1/2 Cup Salt
Salt
Pepper
1/4 Cup Oil
1/2 Stick Butter
2 1/2 Cups Flour (Save 1/2 Cup for Gravy)
1/4 Cup Sherry
1 Teaspoon Liquid Browning Agent

Directions:
Soak quail in 1/2 cup of salt and water overnight. Rinse well. Pat dry. Salt and pepper both sides and cover lightly with flour on both sides.

Brown quail on both sides in oil and butter in a black skillet over medium heat. Remove from skillet and reserve drippings. Place meat in Dutch oven or heavy pan. Cover with gravy made from drippings. Bake for 2 hours at 350 degrees or until tender.

Gravy Directions
In a skillet, place flour in leftover drippings, which should still be hot, and stir with a whisk. Gradually add hot water, stirring briskly with whisk. Continue stirring until well blended. Season to taste with salt and pepper, and then add sherry. Add 1 teaspoon of the liquid browning agent *(this will help to thicken and color gravy)*.

Pheasant
POT PIE

Ingredients
3 Pheasants
4 Tablespoons Salt
Water
1 Onion
2 Stalks Celery
1 Apple, Cut in Wedges
1 Orange, Cut in Wedges
1 Carrot, Cut Up

Pheasant Directions

Cover pheasants in salted water and soak overnight. Drain water, and place pheasants in pot. Rinse, and cover with fresh water.

Cut up onion and celery. Add to the pheasants, along with the apple, orange, and carrot. Cover and boil until pheasant is very tender. Drain, and let meat cool. Remove meat from bone, and cube meat into bite size pieces. Set aside until time to assemble pot pie.

Pie Crust
Ingredients:
4 Cups All Purpose Flour
2 Teaspoons Salt
1 1/2 Cups Shortening
1 Cup Ice Cold Water

Directions:

In mixing bowl, combine flour and salt. Cut in shortening, and add cold water until dough is just moist enough to hold flour together. Place on well floured surface. Work the dough slightly. Divide into 2 balls. Roll out 1 ball of dough, and place into bottom of a 10 x 13 baking dish. Roll out second ball for the top pie crust.

CONTINUED

Vegetable Ingredients
2 Carrots
1 Medium Potato, Peeled and Cubed
1/2 Cup Frozen Peas
1 Medium Onion, Diced

Vegetable Directions
Boil carrots and potatoes in a saucepan for about 5 minutes. Add peas and onions. Let boil for another 2 or 3 minutes. Drain and set aside.

CREAM SAUCE
Ingredients:
6 Tablespoons Butter
6 Tablespoons Flour
2 1/2 Cups Chicken Broth
1 1/2 Cups Whipping Cream
1 Teaspoon Salt
1/2 Teaspoon Pepper
1/2 Teaspoon Thyme, Crushed

Directions:
Combine all ingredients in a saucepan. As sauce heats, stir briskly with a whisk. Continue stirring until sauce thickens. Remove from heat and set aside.

Final Directions
Place cubed pheasant and vegetables in the crust-lined 10 x 13 baking dish. Pour cream sauce over vegetables and meat mixing carefully as not to tear lining of the pie crust.

Place second crust over top of casserole. Make about 6 to 8 small slits in top of crust. Brush top of crust with egg yolk or butter to help brown. In a pre-heated oven, bake at 425 degrees for 25 to 30 minutes or until brown.

Duck
GUMBO

Ingredients

4 Ducks
3 Carrots
3 Stalks Celery
1 Onion
2 Apples
2 Oranges
3 Tablespoons Salt
1 Cup Flour
3/4 Cup Oil
1 Cup Chopped Onion
1 Bunch Chopped Green Onion
1/2 Cup Green Peppers
10 Cups Stock

1/2 Cup Chopped Celery
3 Cloves Minced Garlic
2 Bay Leaves
2 Tablespoons Cajun Seasoning
1/2 Teaspoon Dried Thyme
1 Tablespoon Worcestershire Sauce
1 Tablespoon Tabasco®
1 Pound Cajun Sausage (Sliced)
1 (10 ounce) Box Frozen Okra
4 Cups Cooked Rice
Salt
Pepper

Directions

Place cleaned ducks in a large pot and cover with water. Add cut up carrots, celery (leaves and all), onion, apples, oranges, and salt to taste. Cover, bring to a boil, reduce heat, and simmer for 2 to 3 hours or until meat is tender. Remove ducks and de-bone when cool. Chop meat, and set aside. Strain and save the duck stock.

In a skillet, brown flour and oil, stirring constantly. (To make the roux, this step takes about 20 to 25 minutes. When it is ready, the roux resembles dark chocolate.) Then add chopped onions, green peppers, chopped celery, bay leaves, Cajun seasoning, thyme, Worcestershire Sauce, Tabasco®, and duck stock. Cook over medium heat for 5 minutes, stirring constantly. Slowly add the stock and stir until smooth. Simmer for 2 hours. Add duck meat and Cajun sausage, and simmer for 1 more hour. Add okra, and simmer for 15 minutes. Serve over rice.

Closure

This is the story of a remarkable woman whose love for her family, her craft and her fellow man gave her life meaning and joy. Along the trail of her life, she contined to grow both in spirit and in determination. As her family grew, she imparted a sense of excellence that remains with them today. As her business grew, she afforded several women and men an opportunity to make a living for their families, and to learn a craft that would sustain them throughout the rest of their lives.

Beneva Mayweather's journey through this life ended January 20, 2000, in Memphis, Tennessee. Her culinary journey continues, however, with her husband, children, grandchildren and friends carrying on the work she so dearly loved.

May this cookbook help you to create many wonderful dishes, and may you have as many special memories at your table as we had...

at our Mother's table.

Index

Her Legacy
Continues…